D0998876

THE END.
PART 1

How to write a novel in *BESTSELLER*

30 days

T. STYLES

Copyright © 2012 by The Cartel Publications. All rights reserved.
No part of this book may be reproduced in any form without permission
from the author, except by reviewer who may quote passages
to be printed in a newspaper or magazine.

Any claim of copyright is subject to applicable limitations and
exceptions, such as rights of fair use pursuant to the U.S. Copyright Act.

Printed in the United States of America

While extensive effort has gone into ensuring the reliability of
the information in this book, the publisher makes no warranty,
express or implied, with respect to the material contained herein.

Library of Congress Control Number: 2012930055
ISBN 13: 9780984303090
Cover Design: Davida Baldwin www.oddballdsgn.com
Editor: Advanced Editorial Services
Graphics: Davida Baldwin
www.thecartelpublications.com
First Edition

Printed in the United States of America

PRAISE FOR T. STYLES' NOVELS
Reviews are from Amazon.com

**For the novel 'Quita's DayScare Center' –
(Author Gina West, one of T. Styles' pennames)**
"I read this book in 24 hours. This book was stellar! We finally got to see Quita as a person and not just the Queen of misfits. This story just got better and better with each page. The kids were hilarious and so were the parents. I don't know if Gina West is T.Styles but Ms. West needs a hug or something. Her pen game is on 1000! The Cartel keeps banging out hits and I cannot wait for the next adventure with Quita."

For the novel 'Pitbulls In A Skirt' – (Author is Mikal Malone, one of T.Styles' pennames)
"Pitbulls In A Skirt is an exciting read that captivates the reader with the realistic daily scenes revolving around the central characters. Mikal Malone does a wonderful job of endearing the heroines as they each struggle through troubling situations with their loved ones. The title is indeed trendy yet heartfelt because these four ladies are rare jewels that embody tenacity, strength, steadfastness as well as empower genuine beauty gracefully. Pitbulls In A Skirt is an awesome read! Mikal has most definitely acquired a faithful fan base with this read..."

For the novel 'Shyt List' – (Author is Reign, one of T.Styles' pennames)
"Shyt List is a shocking page-turner by Reign. Reign grabs the reader's attention from the first few pages and doesn't let go until the very end. Readers need to pay close atten-

tion as this story unfolds because things get crazy really fast. This book is full of twisted vendettas and even murder. As you read this novel, you will keep wondering in the back of your mind where Yvonna's father is and why are people suspicious of Yvonna's story about Bilal's murder. There is a jaw-dropping twist that's so jarring, you'll have no clue that it's coming. Shyt List is a fast-paced, thrilling novel that will leave you begging for a sequel from Reign."

For the novel 'Raunchy'

"T. Styles, I must ask if you are okay? What goes on in that head of yours? This book was oh so good! How do you come up with this stuff? I have never read anything like this before and that is a good thing given all the books I have read! Each page is full of drama and action. You will find yourself visualizing exactly what is going on. I CANNOT WAIT for part 2!"

For the novel 'Raunchy 2'

"Last week, I dropped my girlfriend off at work and she left Raunchy 2 in my car. As I was waiting for her to come back with directions to get back home, I flipped the book to the middle (kidnapping) and started reading. Instantly I was hooked, I could NOT put it down. I ended up spending the next 4 hours sitting at my girlfriend's job, in the parking lot, reading the book. Not-to-mention, my girlfriend was shocked I was still there. Lol (laugh out loud) and we spent another 1 1/2 hrs in the parking lot finishing the book.

I ended up rereading the book from the beginning, and I just now purchased this book for my collection.

The book is excellent. I found myself experiencing conflicting emotions between what I feel is morally wrong and *right; and questioning if I have a forgiveness limit. As forgiving as I am, I shocked myself with what I felt was justice (I think I may have shocked my girlfriend too).*

Haven't built up the courage to read Raunchy 1 yet, my girlfriend said it's a lot more graphic and explicit; so it might take me some time to read that one. But as for RAUNCHY 2, GET IT!"

For the short story 'Luxury Tax' from the novel 'Soft'
"I absolutely loved T.Styles' story in this book. The twists, the turns, and the revelations in this book were amazing."

For the novel 'The Face That Launched A Thousand Bullets'
"T. Styles has clearly outdone herself. This book takes the movie Crash and combines it with The Wire and so many other epic movies and stories of our time, all while putting her own poetic spin on this amazing book. There were times while reading this book I literally felt my heart rate speed up and slow down all at the same time. The images painted were so vivid at times I felt myself on those very streets in Bmore (Baltimore). I felt the pain, the pleasure and the sheer gratification and agony that all the characters felt in every chapter. As long as the book was I silently prayed it was longer. 10 Stars for the most EPIC Urban book of the decade thus far."

For the novel 'Miss Wayne & The Queens of DC'
"Ms. Styles pulled me in and out...I could not put this book down. You won't put it down. ...This has made it to my shelf of favorites."

For the novel 'Black & Ugly'

"T. Styles is making me have much respect for her! This story was not your "run of the mill" ghetto story where the girl has the usual tough life, falls for a big time dope dealer and then lives happily ever after following a brush with death. This story touches on a deep issue rooted within the Black community and what many young girls deal with. I love the method of each chapter being a different character's point of view. That really keeps the story moving. This book was filled with action and drama. It was realistic."

For the novel 'Black & Ugly As Ever'

"The sequel was sooo good! I have recently read a sequel that was unnecessary and did nothing to add to the first book. That WAS NOT the case here. I read this in one day! I could not put it down!"

For the novel 'A Hustler's Son'

"T. Styles depicted a young man so well, it makes me wonder about the sex of the author. This was an excellent read."

For the novel 'A Hustler's Son 2'

"I just don't know what to say. But if you love intense reading, please pick up this book and the first one. ...you won't be disappointed. Read in 2 days. ...OMG...just awesome."

For the short story "Cold As Ice" from the novel 'Street Love'

"T. Styles' story Cold As Ice in my opinion was the best. It was very different...not what you expect. ...It was like a movie!"

For the short story "Mona Lisa Dupree" from the novel 'Diamond Playgirls'

"My favorite character was Mona Lisa. She was definitely a go-getta. She was ready to (takeover) with her looks, attitude and mentality. She was detailed and descriptive (on) her character."

ABOUT THE AUTHOR

Toy Styles is a national best selling author. She has authored over 25 successful novels. She runs a popular urban fiction publishing house, The Cartel Publications (www.thecartelpublications.com). She also owns Cartel Book Store and Cartel Urban Cinema, an independent movie company. Although most of her success has been through self publishing, she has gained the attention of the major publishing house Kensington, where her novels have secured mass market deals.

Follow T. Styles:
www.twitter.com/authortstyles
Like Our Cartel Publications FACEBOOK Fan Page
Like T. Styles FACEBOOK Fan Page

DISCLAIMER

**I curse.
A lot.**

TABLE OF CONTENTS

INTRODUCTION

"Welcome to my crazy ass world."
- T. Styles

I never thought I would be a writer. In 2004, it was not a dream of mine. Yet here I am, talking to you about penning your best novel.

I still remember what a psychiatrist told me when I was going through the motions in life. I was in a failed marriage, employed for a company I loved that was relocating my position and I felt all alone. What she told me as I sat across from her was simple. So simple I didn't see how it could possibly work for me. Always the overachiever, I wanted her to give me a blueprint on pulling myself out of depression. Something she was sure would work. Yet she said, *'You should journal, Toy. It may help you relieve some stress."*

"I'm pouring my heart out to you, and you tell me to write in a diary?"

"Trust me, I've seen it work miracles."

With nothing left to lose, I bought a pink book from the drug store and started journaling every single thing that happened in my life. Didn't lead a fulfilling life so the pages were pretty short. At first my entries were boring. I think I was trying to convince myself that I was okay, and that nothing was wrong with me. That I didn't even need a psychiatrist. Over time, with consistency came the truth. I found a need to release stress in my life but I also felt an unnerving desire to tell a story.

By the time I realized I'd written a book, I was forty pages into the story. It got to a point where the things that happened to Evelyn, the main character, weren't even close to my experiences. Before long I had written 150 pages of a novel I penned called *'Rainbow Heart'*. I think I read it over ten times before I could wrap my mind around what I created. Was I officially an author? If I was, I didn't feel like one.

I didn't bother seeking an agent or a publisher when I was done. Besides, who would want to read a book by me? I didn't have anything past a GED and a Certifed Massage Therapy license. I was confused. I didn't know what to do. I mean, I wasn't looking to make it a career, yet the urge to consider the impossible stayed with me always. So when it was complete, sometime in 2005, I published the book myself through a print on demand company called *iUniverse*.

When my manuscript was submitted to the company for printing, I was on edge waiting for the first copy. When it finally arrived, I remember feeling so proud of myself. The support from my friends and a few family members was overwhelming. Part of me was astounded because of the content of the book. I didn't think people would find it interesting or even be able to relate.

After all, Rainbow Heart was about a little girl's struggle to ignore her feelings toward her friend, who was also a girl. Now that I think about it, *originally*, I don't think many people knew what the content was or cared. Because of their support, I sold a few cases and felt proud of myself. Needless to say when I set up book signings, at Barnes and Nobles, I expected the world to be waiting. It didn't happen.

Some time later I was fired from a company I had been employed with for over five years. All my life I had a job. Based on the social security statements I receive every so often, I should be able to live comfortably if I were to retire today. Now there I was, unemployed. Who was I if I wasn't working for a large company? Who was I if I couldn't afford to take care of my family? Since I come from a line of strong women, in my opinion, I was a bum.

I was completely lost and outside of my first book, I didn't have a plan of action to earn money. Glancing at *Rainbow Heart*, which sat on my table, next to my bed, I wondered if I could make a career out of writing, even though the success of my first title had been less than favorable.

With nothing left to lose, I decided to take a chance and write another book. Remembering most of my ex-coworkers enjoyed urban fiction; I researched small publishing houses in that genre. At the time, *Triple Crown Publications* was the house you wanted to go to, if you wanted a chance at success. The writers in that house, K'wan, Nikki Turner, Tushonda Whitaker, Keisha Ervin, all made names for themselves and I looked up to them. I still do.

Frustrated and jobless, I wrote the synopsis for a book I hadn't written called *Mama's Soldier*. Per their guidelines I sent it in, and immediately they contacted me wanting to read the book. I remember trembling when I saw the name Triple Crown Publications, on my caller ID. Everybody in my family gave me my space and was very supportive. This was a chance to change the world as we saw it and they welcomed the opportunity. I felt blessed to have such a tight unit.

Quickly I wrote the requested title and to be sure I got a deal, I wrote another novel titled *Black & Ugly*, about a young lady who does not appreciate her dark skin. Two weeks later, I got my book deal.

It didn't take long for the honeymoon to be over. I soon realized that *Triple Crown Publications* was a disastrous company to write for. Checks constantly bounced, they reported incorrect income to the IRS and in my opinion, they didn't respect their authors. All I wanted to do was get out of the deal I made with the devil, and write for a reputable company so that I could feed my family. There was one problem. Per my agreement, until I fulfilled my contractual obligations, I could not write another book under my own name.

Thinking on my feet I realized that although Vickie Stringer could slow down my process, she couldn't kill my dreams or talent. Besides, I had a family to support and I realized that I could supplement my income by being a writer if, and this is important, I wrote a *great* book. Not a book of trash, but a book of entertainment and enjoyment. I also discovered that I loved the art of telling stories. It was my life.

So, I thought of a concept for two other novels. One was titled *Shyt List* (pronounced Shit List) and the other was *The Promise of A Hustler*. Using the pen names Reign and Mikal Malone, I penned both novels within 30 days.

Immediately I sought publishing houses, and at the time, no one wanted to bite. Partially because of the presence *Triple Crown Publications* had in the industry, and because I needed to be secretive when promoting my books if they gave me an opportunity. Remember, I couldn't write a book because I was still under contract under my own name. I had to be honest when seeking publishers, explaining to them that although T. Styles was tied up, Reign and Mikal Malone were fully prepared to promote the titles if given a chance. No one was interested.

After a few more months of dealing with *Triple Crown Publications*, I realized I needed to push off and start my own publishing house. What titles did I use to launch my label? *Shyt List* and *Pitbulls In A Skirt*, previously titled, *A Promise of A Hustler*. Many years later, the same books rejected by other publishing houses, have consistently profited my own house. Now I have mass-

THE END. PART 1

market deals with major publishing houses for those exact titles.

I had no experience writing. I have a GED. I never took a writing class in my life. And yet, I am a full time author/publisher. Everything I've learned along the way, has been obtained by reading books in this craft. Lots of books! So can you write a novel in 30 days? Absolutely! Is there something you must do above all? Yes! And we are going to talk about those things in this book. But it is important to understand that although I can give you the tools I use to bang out best sellers, reading this book will not afford you the same successes, or even better, greater successes, if you don't apply the techniques.

It is also important to understand that I'm not an editor. I'm a writer and the positions are two different things. I know how to teach you to construct your best work because I've been doing it successfully for years. But you'll have to select your own editor to perfect your work. By the end of this book, if you give me your undivided attention, you will have perfected it too.

CHAPTER ONE
A Little Book Is Murdered

First off this book is for procrastinators. The writers who have a dream, but don't know how to flesh it out. If you have a process that works for you, I don't suggest you read this book. Knowing myself I'm going to go against everything you've been taught, and you'll be frustrated. I repeat, this book is not for the uptight folks or the writers who think they know it all. Nobody knows it all. Life is about learning and growth. I'm not going to convince you of anything, nor do I want to. I'm going to be discussing some unconventional ideas, including ditching outlines early on. Now if I haven't scared you off yet, this book is for you.

Why do some writers have a hard time writing a book? Because they make it harder than it has to be. Actually, as writers, we all do. For more reasons than not, we have a sincere desire to make things perfect, when perfect is impossible. You should always strive for your best, leave perfect to doctors. Your best is easier and achievable.

I get you because I was the same at the onset of my career. I wanted to be all I could be and as quickly as possible. The problem was, I spent too much time on learning the art of setting up a story and I didn't realize how important it was to enjoy myself in the process. Now after many years of being in the business, I'm realizing that unless you enjoy telling stories, you can't be good at it. It's like a chef who doesn't like to cook but is in charge of dinner. If you are unlucky enough to eat one of his meals, the food would be bland and lifeless. You must love this craft if you are going to write a bestseller. Get into it for any other reason, and you're doomed.

Reading books should be joyous and so should writing them. In fact, there shouldn't be a writer alive who doesn't enjoy reading novels. Reading great books is one of the reasons you decide to be a writer. Think about it for a minute. You read a great novel, it called to your soul and immediately you're inspired. Before long you say to yourself, *'I can write a book as good as that author or better!'* You decide at that moment to recreate the same feeling when someone picks up your book. And if you are lucky, you hope to replicate the same success. You don't stop to think about your biggest problem...YOU! Allow me to take you through what *really* happens, the moment you decide to fulfill your dreams.

First, you have a great idea for your own novel. You make up your mind to tell your story which, most of the time, embodies large parts of your personal life. When you sit down to get started, the first page flows effortlessly. You take a brief look at yourself, the way your fingers move so 'writer like' and you feel elated. You can't believe you are really about to do this shit. You're really about to write a fucking book!

When you reach the second page, your motivation may not be as strong as when you first started, but you try your best to remain focused. After a few more minutes of *faking it*, you make an excuse that today is not the best day to start, so you call it quits for the moment. You're not worried though, because you tell yourself you'll be back the next day. Besides, you promised to make the chicken that thawed out in the kitchen sink, and your beans are soaking in the refrigerator. Your family will be coming home soon and they're going to want dinner.

As you prepare your meal, you get on the phone and call a few friends to tell them about your new mission, to become a published author. You suggest that they save any card you've given them over the years, because before long, your signature will be worth millions. After all, you're about to be the next big thing.

The next day comes soon enough and you force yourself to get in the mind frame. You read somewhere that writing an outline might help, but you're not sure where to start. You grab your notebook, walk it to the kitchen table and pull out your chair. Sitting down, you examine the book before you write and open it slowly.

'*It's really about to happen*', you tell yourself. Wasting no more time you flip the book open and look at the last page you wrote on. Suddenly you realize you don't like your penmanship. In your opinion it isn't legible and it worries you. I mean what were you doing, writing with your feet? If you're going to be a famous writer you're going to have to start from the top. This sort of writing is totally unacceptable as far as you're concerned. '*Nobody is going to be able to read this shit*', you say, pulling the page out. '*I'm gonna start all over. Besides, I just started and have plenty of time.*'

You ball it up and toss it toward the trashcan. It doesn't make it and instead, it lands next to the can. In your opinion it's some strange Omen. If your rough draft can't even make the trash, what makes you think your novel will make it in the major leagues? Having played this game before with your mind, you shake your head, smile and get to work. You're smarter than these mind games so you tell yourself you must stick to your goal. You want it that badly!

Your pen so eloquently moves across the page that you can already see the lines around the corner at Barnes and Noble. And then your phone rings. You place your pen down, scoot away from the chair and move toward the handset. The only reason you answer is because you're

THE END. PART 1

going to tell whoever is calling to get lost. You don't need them interrupting your work again. But when you answer the phone, it's your best friend calling to tell you that the *What's Going Down* episode of *That's My Mama*, is on TV. Surely you can't miss this show. After all, what are the chances of it coming on again?

So you neatly tuck your work away in your dresser, with empty promises to give it all you have next week. You would start again tomorrow, but you're taking your mother to the concert to see Aretha Franklin. Saturday will simply have to do. You tell yourself you are just busy and not making excuses. When in all actuality, you're making more excuses than a guilty man going to jail.

Saturday finds you soon enough and you made the mistake of telling an unsupportive friend about your book. They look at you as if your wig was sliding backwards and fell on the floor. At that moment you begin to question yourself and your talent. *Who am I to even think that I could write a book? The nerve of me to think that I could be something bigger than what I am.*

You make a discovery at that moment. You tell yourself that while you are a good mother, father, or friend, you will never be an author. You tell yourself its okay. Besides, being famous would be too much anyway. Who needs all the extra attention? Surely not you. You adore your privacy. You are destined to be a nine to fiver and that's the bottom line. So you grab the paper holding the first line of your dream and wipe your ass with it. Just like that, your aspirations of being a writer are gone and so is your novel. You murdered your book, by yourself.

Were there some things you could have done to prevent this pitfall? Yes. For starters you need to understand what being a writer means. It means you will open yourself up to scrutiny from the people you love, and the people whose attention you hope do attract to your story.

If you are the kind of person to give up so easily, you will not have any success in this industry. You have to be strong to be a writer. You're going to have to be selfish, and even unkind at times when you run into those who mean to stop you from achieving your dream. You are going to have to muster the strength to let no one stand in your way, and give your ass to kiss to those who don't get the picture. Oh yes, you will have to be an unconscionable ass at times, but after awhile, people will get the picture and get out of your way, or get run over.

Once you have scared off every last fake family member and friend in your life, those who are standing around you when the smoke clears will be all you need. Take a good look at them. They are the people who you've expressed your desire to be something greater than yourself and they are still around. They are far from haters. This is your team, and you need to respect them as much as possible.

What does that mean? It means that you can't forget about them along the way. It means you have to make a schedule and stick to it so that you can spend time with them. It means that when you're outside of this schedule, you need to give your family members and friends the love they require.

Don't worry, I'm going to stick with you every step of the way, but first lets talk about how to use this book.

CHAPTER TWO
How To Use This Book

"Put in the time."
-Sue Grafton

The End. was intended as a companion tool to be used in my seminars. Originally I was not going to publish this book but decided to do so, after many writers requested. Although this book can help you formulate a plan to write your novel in a short time, if you can attend one of my seminars, I really suggest you do so. At the seminars I am on hand to help you with specific issues that may be plaguing your work, and participants leave with the first five pages of their novel complete. Register in the support group below, to find out about upcoming dates.

Still, this book is designed to help you create your novel by motivating you and providing you with an interesting process. A different process. An unconventional process. I am a rebel and because of it, I break rules. This one trait allows me to break molds and push standards, and you will too. This book is unlike any you've read because I'm not interested in teaching you about your verbs and dangling participles. I don't mean for you to ignore the basic foundations of formatting sentences, but they aren't needed to write your book in 30 days. You'll eventually need a strong editor for that. Still, I am going to give you a process that works that is not necessarily about obeying the English standards.

How do I know, because I write two to three books at a time within a 30-day time frame. And every single step presented in this book, I use. I have learned from trial and error what works, and what doesn't. You will learn and be able to apply the tools if you stick to my instructions. You've tried your way and it didn't work. You found yourself all over the place at times, so you have to have an open mind and follow this regimen to a T.

It's not enough to pen a novel if your thoughts, ideas and focus are all over the place. Anybody can place a bunch of words on a paper and call it a book. However, your book will only be as good as your ideas (which I can't give you) and my process, which I can provide. You have to dig in your mind and come up with new and amazing ideas and this book will help you formulate them once you do.

You read a lot so you have a pretty good idea about what works and what doesn't work in a book. If you can remember, think of the things you've despised when trying to enjoy a book and avoid them at all cost when writing your novel. Those small irritations will be your savings graces if you take heed on how you felt.

Although we discuss a lot, before we begin the 30-day countdown, this book is primarily a companion to keep you focused throughout your journey. So you will open this book on the day you begin, and for everyday afterwards, until your novel is complete.

You should always refer to this book, whenever you first start a NEW novel. The daily process will help you remember the techniques and PREPARE before you start your journey. The messages are geared to assist you so that this time will be different and you'll achieve your goal. Although I suggest using every tool I offer, I place jewels next to the items I want you to pay close attention to. I love diamonds! Don't you?

To ensure that you have support, you will join the *THE END* writers group

THE END. PART 1

http://groups.yahoo.com/group/theendnovelin30days/. This group is also designed to support you from day one until the 30th day of your process. Afterwards, you may still use this forum to speak with other alumni. Please sign up and get to know other writers who are also walking the road to attain their goals. It is so much easier when you have support.

In addition, at the end of each week, you will receive an email from me giving you encouragement as you reach your goal. Please take a moment to read the emails, as they will always seem to come when you need them the most. To register for my emails please sign into the group above.

Finally, on the last day of each month, (if it falls on a holiday the call will be hosted the following day) I will host a call to keep you inspired. Call 712-432-0075 pin# 478471 at 7:00pm eastern. I highly recommend you listen in on the call no matter where you are in your journey. I sincerely want to see your dreams realized, and I believe these tools combined, will help lead the way.

I also have compiled an amazing list of resources that you may refer to no matter where you are in your career. The list alone is a reason to keep this book closely by your side because you will find all of the links valuable.

This book is a work of love. I truly gave you every tool I utilize to effectively and smoothly assist you in writing your novel. I'm not speaking from hearsay, or quoting the pages of someone else's book (notwithstanding author quotes). Although I might refer to something that is common knowledge amongst writers, the way in which I use them are my own.

There is no reason to mull over a book for years at a time. Don't believe a person when they say writing your best book is not achievable in a year. It is achievable in a few months! I want you to get your first novel done so that you can go about the business of living. Just because you chose to live out your dreams and be an author, does not mean it should consume every waken moment of your life. By using this book and being organized and motivated, you will soon realize your strengths and rid yourself of your weaknesses. And above all, don't forget to have fun.

CHAPTER THREE
Preparation Makes Perfect!

"The 30 day countdown starts after you prepare."
- T. Styles

First things, first! The 30 days begin, AFTER you prepare. In my opinion, the preparation stage takes five days. You can take less, but never take more. I know some of you are already feeling defeated because you're eager to start and I appreciate your energy. However, Brooklyn was not built in a day and neither will your book. Others of you may be saying, *'Let me try another way to write my book, because it may be easy for T. Styles to write a book in 30 days. She's been writing for years. But what about me?'*

I'm not going to lie, the finesse that it takes to get better at this craft will develop over time. I didn't slide out of my mother's pussy knowing how to write a book. (Forgive my potty mouth. I tried to have it cleaned.) In fact, outside of obtaining a GED, taking a few college courses in foolery and becoming a certified massage therapist, I don't have what some may consider, education in this field. I'm self-taught in this game yet I've obtained a level of success. And one of my secrets is being prepared before I sit down to create. Before you enter T. Styles' boot camp, you must get your tools together. And it starts with having a conversation with your close friends and close family.

THE CONVERSATION

"Writing is like sex. You should do it, not talk about it."
-Howard Ogden

To write a book you must FIRST write word one. We can't play around with the idea of penning a novel, you should just do it. I was told by *A GREAT*, that boxers, box and writers write. But, as with anything we have to set the stage first. If you notice earlier, I wrote that you should tell *close* friends and *close* family members. Why? Because some people will try to sabotage your success and we don't want them to be apart of your process. When you make it big and become a bestselling author, insecure people may base their failures off your successes and become resentful towards you. You don't need this energy around you when you're creating. In order to write your best, you need the most comfortable working environment possible.

FAMILY & FRIENDS

There are two groups of family members and friends. The Care Family & Friend Members, which we'll call CFF's and the Extended Family & Friend Members, which we'll call EFF's.

CFF's are those who rely on you for care and attention. They are your husbands, wives, children, best friends and any person living in your home. They see or talk to you everyday, and simply ignoring them while you complete your project may not be conducive. You may find yourself in a worse condition than you started, which is not what we want. Remember, you need a clear mind and peaceful heart. Like I said earlier, CFF's can also be those members that you speak to on a regular basis. Because although you may not be responsible for their everyday well-being, (meals, homework, etc.) they may still depend on you for emotional support. In order to complete your book, you will need as balanced of a state as possible. CFF's are going to need an explanation on why you'll be disconnected when you begin your process. So be cautious when speaking to them.

The EFF's are those members who you may speak to a few times a month. These members, although still apart of your family and friends, should not be privy to a conversation. You know who they are. They're five conversations away from being straight haters. Simply tell them that you may be busy but you'll contact them when you can. The group I want to focus on are the CFF's.

You don't need to tell CFF's what your book is about. Besides, you might not have any idea of what your book is about and it's all good. You've *talked* about doing things in the past, and most of those projects never got off the ground. And if you tell your CFF's about the intrinsic details of your story, you might read into their body language incorrectly and become discouraged. You may feel that they think your idea is a joke. You don't need this. We're artists and we're sensitive about our shit, even if we haven't written anything yet. Let's talk about the conversation with the CFF's.

The conversation example I'm going to give you below is not meant to make you feel like a juvenile. Sometimes we think too hard when less is more. When you have the conversation with your CFF's, it should go a little something like this:

"I've decided to write a book and I'm going to officially start on April 1ˢᵗ. Dinner will be prepared most nights but if you can help me every so often, I would really appreciate it. I plan to write every evening."

"Well how long do you think it will take?"

"The initial process will take 30 days. I'm really excited! Can I count on your support?"

You're asking for support because you want them to feel a part of the process. Of course you can tailor your conversation depending upon whom you're speaking with, but the specifics are the same. You need to give them the date you plan to start and how long your initial process will last. The reason? You are imprinting on your subconscious that you are about to begin a new journey, and you have put it out in the universe. Now people are going to see if you are really serious and sometimes, that alone gives us the energy to follow through.

Of course if they say they do not support you, feel free to tell them to fuck off. No...I'm just kidding. Well actually I'm serious. Nobody, and I do mean nobody, should give up on his or her dream, especially for those who mean to stand in your way. Even if you have to spend hours a day *using the bathroom writing*, let nothing or no one separate you from this goal. This time MUST BE DIF-FERENT! You have to be relentless and over time, if nothing else, they will learn to respect you. But even if they don't, and this is real, you must learn to not care. You don't want years to pass you by, only to wonder if you could've achieved your dream.

If you are in charge of dinner, during this period, you need to plan meals that are easy to prepare. If you can, make enough for leftovers the next day so you will give yourself a break. I enjoy making spaghetti, lasagna, Frito Pie which is ground beef with taco seasoning, over rice and cheddar cheese. Sprinkle Fritos around it and there you go. If you are on a restricted diet, during the five-day period, think about meals that will last a few days. Last but not least, ask your spouse or older children to help you out with meals. After all, when your book is a success, every-

THE END. PART 1

one will benefit from the process so everyone should lend support.

Who are the CFF's in your life?

_____

_____

_____

_____

_____

_____

Who are the EFF'S in your life?

_____

_____

_____

_____

_____

What quick meal ideas can you make to buy more time during your journey?

_____

_____

_____

_____

_____

THE UNSUPPORTIVE SPOUSE

This chapter may hurt, but it will be quick. Because truthfully, I'm telling you something you already know. You may have someone in your life who doesn't want you to achieve great things. They will try to thwart your success at every chance. These people may move this way for different reasons. Maybe they are afraid to achieve anything themselves, and watching you reach for your goals will bring their own weaknesses to light. Maybe they are afraid of losing you, if you become successful. Whatever the reason, it can be depressing for the artist who just wants to tell stories and entertain.

I was in a relationship like this and it was hell. He showed me on a repeated basis that he didn't want me to succeed, even though he said he did. He was cunning and knew if he came out and said, *I don't want you to be your best*, I would've walked out with the quickness. Instead, he picked fights when I was in the throws of a story. When my mind was on penning my best work.

For instance, he'll say something that he knew would set me off. Any other time I would attack, but when writing I wouldn't respond because I valued my creative energy. Instead I would try to reassure him that I loved him, and ignore the attempt to cause an argument altogether. He'd still bicker and I would beg him to not upset my flow. If I even implied that I believed he was trying to prevent me from writing, he would act standoffish and avoid me all together, which was also stressful. Because now I would have to worry if he was getting love from somebody else. This hurt because I thought I wanted the relationship.

These types of men and women are dangerous to the hopeful author, so I'm going to be real with you. You cannot be in an unhealthy relationship and be successful for long. You can't do anything worthwhile in an unhealthy relationship. I'm so sorry. I wish I could tell you that there was some way to get them to change. I wish I could give you some magic verse to make them supportive overnight. Perhaps remaining focused on your work and not giving up on your dreams will facilitate the process. However, it did not work for me. In the end I left the relationship and did not look back.

You are going to lose friends and relationships on your pursuit. However, the people who you cut off while you move toward your goal, needed to be gone anyway. You can't continue to live for someone else. It's unhealthy and unfair. There will come a time when you'll have to weigh what is more important to you. Being a writer might be what you needed all along, to give you an excuse to demand respect in your life and clean house.

A peaceful environment and a calm spirit is a necessity to all writers. I certainly don't want you to make any drastic decisions now, by ending any relationships. I want you to be as stress free as possible. However, I do want you to be assessing your circle at all times, to make sure its round, and not dented.

Do you have an unsupportive spouse? If so, what can you do to avoid conflict, as you prepare to make your goal?

_____
_____
_____
_____
_____
_____
_____

TOOLS OF THE TRADE

"There's a word for a writer who never gives up. Published."
- Joe Konrath

So you've had the conversation. Now what's next? It's time to gather the tools of the trade. Below is a list of devices that I swear by, especially when I'm first beginning to create a masterpiece. Ladies and gentlemen I introduce to you, T. STYLES' LIST!

T.STYLES' LIST

- 1 Great nonfiction book (I recommend The Book of Awakening by Mark Nepo)
- 1 GREAT book (In the genre you're writing your novel)
- 1 GREAT pen
- 1 Notebook with perforated pages inside
- 1 Box of manila folders
- 1 Pack of Post-It Self-Stick easel pad sheets 25 x 30 (or somewhere close)
- 1 Pack of colorful markers (I favor the Sharpie chart markers, not the fine point)
- 1 Small pad or note recording machine. (I use the note application in my iPhone)
- Colorful Markers
- Arthritis gloves

PURPOSE OF TOOLS

 Great Non Fiction Book

A great non-fiction book is essential to your success. So for five minutes a day, I'll need you to read out of one. As of now you're probably saying, *'Toy, come on...you want me to read and write a book?'* Yes! Think of it like training before the training. If you were a boxer, even if you're sparring, you wouldn't jump in the ring without preparing. You'll do a few stretches, maybe even some lunges so that you'll warm the body up but you won't jump your stiff ass in the ring with no practice. Unless you want to get knocked on your ass. So, the purpose of a great non-fiction book is to clear some of the emotional baggage in your mind you've collected along the way. Maybe you got into an argument with a friend...or a boss. Whatever your problem, you want to clear it as much as possible before you write, by getting into a positive frame of mind.

If you are emotionally pulled in other directions, which many of you are, you will need to fill your cup with positivity before setting about the business to create. A lot of people don't realize how important peace is and because of it, they find it hard to get into the zone. I know this is probably what you don't want to hear, but trust me when I say it is necessary to read positive books.

The reason I prefer the *Book of Awakening,* as opposed to any other novel, is because of the way the book is formatted. It gives you daily food for thought and you read it based on the day of the month. The passages are not too long so you don't have to worry about spending all of your creative energy on reading. In my opinion, it is also non denominational so it does not intrude on any one belief. Taking a few minutes to read the quick passages before I start writing, leaves me with the feeling that I can accomplish anything. And in my mind and heart, I'm sure this translates to my reader when my novel is complete.

Great Fiction Book
For fifteen minutes a day, you are also to read a fiction book. I don't care what people say, if you don't read, you can't become a great writer. Even if you have a pretty good career without reading other novels now, if you don't take the time to read stories in your genre, at some point you will suffer burn out. Many of my peers may disagree with me but it is fact. It has been proven by the greats, including Stephen King, that to write great books you have to read. Notice I said you have to *read* as opposed to read *great* books. Let me explain.

When you start your journey, I'm going to need you to select books that are the best of the best. Read reviews, talk to a few of your friends who enjoy reading and do your best to select books you can grow from. Why? Because reading *great* books will inspire you to put out your best. You are not to plagiarize, attempt to copy the author's style or technique. It will be fruitless anyway. You must develop your own. Be your own person. The world has enough fakes and frauds.

Reading great books for no less than fifteen minutes a day is simply a way to motivate you even more. It's similar to going to church every Sunday, which is the start of the week. You are doing this to be inspired to have the best week possible. Now if you read a bad book, you may feel discouraged and will likely not complete your journey. You may even call the writer and curse him or her out.

However, once you become a pro, and you will become a professional, you must complete every book you start reading. This includes the bad ones. Why? Because there is no such thing as a worthless book. You will learn as much from the bad books as you will from the great ones, if you keep an open mind.

Overtime, you will force yourself not to repeat the same mistakes so that your book will become respected by readers near and far. You will find it very difficult to finish awful books, I'm not going to lie, but you must stick to it when the time comes. You must study and understand what makes good books great and bad books awful. Take notes if you have to, and create cheat sheets for yourself. If you remain conscious of this process overtime you will become a great.

Pen & Paper

The best tool a serious writer could ever have is a good pen and paper. I'm not going to waste your time. We all know what the pen is used for as well as paper. What you probably don't understand is the importance of having the best. Having a great pen ties into the reason I don't want you to use a computer…at first anyway.

In order for you to get the process done in 30 days, you need minimal distractions. If you are disconnected from the Internet on your computer, and you are fluent in the word processing application of your choice, type away. However, if you are connected to the net I insist you take it back to caveman days.

I use a *Cross* fountain pen and *Noodlers* ink in black. When I use these tools, I feel invincible and prestigious and that energy comes across in my work. Its as if I'm summoning the great writers of the 10th century, totally before my time. Not only that, but by using a fountain pen and by having my ink available, I don't run the risk of being in the mode, only to have to use another pen because I'm out of ink. When my ink runs out, I simply refill it and go about my work. I am always prepared.

I'm not requesting that you purchase a forty-dollar pen, even though I do, especially if you are use to giving your pen away in the grocery store and forgetting to get it back. However, I will demand that you buy a pen you feel comfortable working with. A pen that will allow your words to spill across the paper, never missing a curve. A great pen will add respect to your craft and, if you get the right one, will last forever.

I touched on the importance of using paper as opposed to a computer earlier but I'll mention it again here. It is imperative that this time when you sit down to write your book, that your process be different. If you sit in front of a computer connected to the Internet, my concerns are many.

First you'll log on your computer with all intentions of avoiding the Internet. You may try harder, by disabling the Wi-Fi. However your phone which is sitting next to you, with a full Internet connection in tact, is still available. Eventually it will ding indicating you have a text message, and you'll pick it up to respond. Somehow after reading the message, you'll receive a non-related notification that someone messaged you on Facebook. So what do you do...you log on there.

You discover that someone attached something to your page, which you're very overprotective of, and now you must delete it right away. Before deleting the unsolicited post on your page, you notice that a friend is having a baby and that another friend is throwing her a surprised shower. You RSVP, because you don't want to miss it for anything in the world. Plus the friend throwing the party always buys good food and liquor.

Remembering the message that was waiting for you, you read it and immediately grow angry. Your associate is accusing you of not being a friend, and that she's going to cut you off because you're two faced. You get into a heated battle with her right on the spot, before eventually picking up the phone to call her at home. You call her a bitch, curse her out, and hang up in her face. Now your emotions are riled up and you wonder why you logged on Facebook to begin with. Had you kept your mind on your book, none of this would've happened.

So you walk over to the Internet router, yank it out of the wall and slam yourself back into your seat and try to get some work done. It doesn't go over well because now you're thinking about all the people she's probably talking to. You need to tell your side before lies infect your little circle.

You get the picture right? If you didn't know before you will learn early on that it is impossible to write effectively and efficiently with your mind all over the place. This is why I mentioned in the introductions that you need to get your house in order and read books to keep you focused. Moral of the story? Stay away from the Internet and stick to the pen and pad. Put that phone on silent too. You'll save your project and the last few brain cells you have left.

Your notebook is just as important as your pen. You must choose one that speaks to you. Although I don't have a preference in regards to a brand of notebook, I do prefer if you choose one with a positive motivational message on the front. You don't have to be as corny as me, (mine says, *sometimes the best man for the job is a woman*) but you must choose one you like. I don't care if it has Beyoncé on the front of it or a Gremlin. Pick one that calls your name.

The object is to always get tools you love because when you do you'll cherish them and they'll inspire your work. God truly is in the details, and these simple steps to some may seem trivial, but may mean the difference from writing a bestseller, to nursing over a book for two to three years. Besides, your notebook will soon hold the pages of your national best seller. Wouldn't you want it written in a book you love?

Box of Manila Folders

Your notes, your reminders, your ideas and eventually the first copy of your book in 30 days, should all be kept in a manila folder. On the front of the folder should be the name of your book and you must also cherish this folder with all your might. Get into the habit of putting everything related to your book inside of it. Organization truly is the vehicle necessary to write a best seller. It is impossible to be effective unless everything pertaining to your book is in a central location.

As your bibliography grows, you will be able to refer to your folders if need be. Imagine how seamless it will be to have immediate access to your notes if you decide to write spin offs or sequels to your stories. No longer will you have to read the entire book again (although I do) before penning a sequel. Using the manila folders and having an organized state of mind is how you win.

Pack of Post-It Self-Stick easel pad sheets 25 x 30

Some people are visual and I am one of those people. Done correctly, the large Post It Notes will neatly display your characters, their traits, as well as the locations involved in your book. They are the sheets that usually go on easels. Where will the Post-It's be? On your wall. This will come in handy when you form rewrites and will save time so you won't have to always scan your story to find an answer regarding your characters.

Since we're speaking about rewrites, let me just jump out there and say that the book you'll write in 30 days is only your rough draft. You will not go to press with this book, love. Don't get discouraged, because we'll revisit this again later.

The Post It notes, which will be stuck to the wall in your writing space, will allow you to see who your characters are while you're creating scenes. This tool is probably one of my favorites, as it came to me later in my career. No more having to look through my papers to remember how a character looks or behaves. Your lists will include important minor characters as well. You will find that you will refer to this chart often when your process begins.

Starting out, you will use three sheets. One for your main characters, minor characters and locations. As you become comfortable with this process, please make it your own and add more sheets if necessary. But, DO NOT OVERWHELM YOURSELF! This tool should be helpful, not a hindrance.

If you don't have enough space to place the Post It's on the wall in your bedroom, what about your closet? If you can find a space that is your own, I really want you to take advantage of it. If space is definitely a problem, and you don't want your family members reading your business, you may use notebook paper. The idea is to have a quick reference to refer to your characters throughout the time you are writing your book.

Using a fictitious novel title, *Bad Pop Bad Cop*, I will show you how to use the Post It sheets.

MAJOR CHARACTER SHEET			
	Shelly	**Todd**	**Mark**
Age	18	55	32
Hair	Long black hair	Bald head	Low haircut – black hair
Height	5'5	6'0	6'1
Weight	140 pounds	220 pounds	180 pounds
Job	College Dropout	Retired Veteran	Police Officer
Weaknesses	Trusts too easily. Relies on father for everything. Is afraid of heights. Lonely. Desires love.	Drunk. Verbally abusive when under the influence. Stays out late at night. Sleeps with other women.	Arrogant. Power trips. Cares too much about what people think. Sneaky
Strengths	Loves family. Trustworthy.	A provider.	An officer. Coaches special needs children.
Relationship Status	Single	Married	Dates various women.

*Hint
You will not need to use every characteristic when writing your story. For instance you don't have to say, Shelly was 5'5 and 140 pounds. The idea of the chart is to help you to get to know your characters better, visually.

THE END. PART 1

LOCATION SHEET			
AMC Movie Theater	Shonda's Hair Salon	Candy's Bar & Grill	Todd's Living Room
Todd's Bedroom	Todd's Bathroom	Todd's Kitchen	Todd's Dining Room
Todd's Backyard	Shelly's Bedroom	Angie's Bedroom	Mark's Living Room
Mark's Bedroom	Mark's Car	The Precinct	Mark's Bathroom

* Hint:
It is not a requirement to have a note sheet. However, if you believe it will be easy to store your notes on a large POST IT, as opposed to notebook paper, I prefer you to utilize this tool. The note sheet is used to place items you want in your book, after you've already finished the chapter. This is key because the idea is to avoid rewrites. By placing your items here, you are free to come back to it after you finish the first draft.

NOTE SHEET			
Have Shelly call her best friend in chapter two _____	Make Mark call off for work in chapter three		

Major Character Sheet

The major character sheet is self-explanatory. Going across the top you want your main characters names. Vertically you want the following sections:

Age
Hair-which includes style and color
Height
Job
Weaknesses
Strengths
Relationship Status

You can also add a section for the following:

Hobbies and Physical Quirks

This sheet is a jewel. Trust me. Now when you get stuck, you simply have to raise your head, look at your sheet and see who your characters are. This sheet may change with your story but you can update it as needed, or replace it with a whole new one AFTER you write your rough draft. Remember, you are not to do any rewrites prior to birthing a rough draft.

Location Sheet

Location sheets are meant to give you a place to take your reader. Don't underestimate the power of location. Personally I enjoy having as many locations as possible. Think of it this way. Imagine if someone was in charge of your life. And every day you wake up, although they may bring people to visit you, they keep you in the house. Eventually

THE END. PART 1

you will get bored and wonder what goes on in the world outside.

Location sheets are a quick way to not only place your major locations, but to also give you a little nudge while creating scenes on the spur. Maybe you want to create a cool love scene, but the bedroom doesn't stimulate you. Look at your location sheet and pick a new place to create a passionate affair. Maybe even in a public place, like a bathroom or car!

Think of some cool locations. Write them here:

_____
_____
_____
_____
_____
_____
_____
_____
_____
_____
_____
_____

Colorful Markers
Your colorful markers will be used on the Post It Notes. Please keep each character color-coded as shown above. It is okay to use the same color you use on a minor character, for a major character. However, do not use the same colors on the same sheet. All characters on the Major sheet should have different colors, etc. It is important to adopt a military state of mind as you move toward your goal.

Arthritis Gloves
You must care for your hands. You are a writer and your hands are important to your success. Although you don't need your hands to write a book, because of the voice recognition tools available today, if typing is your primary method, you need to protect your equipment. One of my favorite tools are arthritis gloves. Wear them even if your hands aren't giving you trouble now.

Although there are many on the market, I prefer *IMAK* Arthritis Gloves. The reason I prefer the cotton gloves as opposed to the carpal tunnel gloves is because they are too bulky for me. *IMAK* gloves are cotton, gray and have black rims along the edges of the finger holes. My hands stay warm and comfy. They provide mild compression, and my fingers are free and not restricted. Whether you use carpal tunnel gloves or arthritis gloves, it is imperative that you use them EVERYDAY. No exceptions. Consult your physician and choose the best option for you.

 **Small Notepad or the Note recording machine on your phone**
In my opinion this small step is CRUICIAL! As you move about life you will encounter new people, new scenarios and new things, which will spark your creativity. When you do, you need to jot them down in your recording op-

tion **IMMEDIATELY**! And if you think you will remember these little gifts from God, you are dead wrong! I repeat, you will not remember what you see, hear and smell out in the world because I've tried it and I always fail.

At the point this book was written, I penned over 25 novels and to this day, I cannot find a better way to remember my ideas than placing them in my iPhone, the moment I get the idea. Why risk losing your awesome ideas when it takes seconds to record them? Please don't ignore this advice, as it will be one of the most important things I've said to you thus far. Over time you will accumulate ideas that will help you avoid writer's block and you will need to refer to your list.

If you've followed my career, you know that in interviews I explain that I do not suffer writers block. My reason? Because I have amassed over fifty pages of ideas since I've started my career. I don't let one idea pass me by. In fact, my friends and family are so use to me recording every interesting thing I see, that they call me when things happen in their lives. They know that as long as they have me, the wild moments that go on around them will not go to waste.

It is also important to do more listening than talking when you are out and about. The world has enough talkers. Don't be one of those people. Be a great listener! Everybody has something to say and they love to be heard. If you can't get into the habit of opening your eyes and ears, you will never be able to fulfill your dreams. We are the recorders of life. You have to be aware of people, their actions, what they're wearing, how they interact with one another and how they feel. Through developing this unique skill, and implementing it in your work, you allow people to see how ridiculous, loving, funny, hateful, and happy they are in your books.

Recording your ideas is not an option. It is the *ONLY* option. If you don't begin to do this now, you will not have the fuel necessary to push yourself when writing your book gets rough. And it will get rough.

Did anything happen interesting to you today? If so, record it here:

_____

_____

_____

_____

_____

_____

_____

_____

_____

_____

_____

_____

_____

_____

_____

CHAPTER FOUR
You Are To Write A Character Driven Book, Not The Other Way Around

"If you have other things in your life-family, friends, good productive day work-these things can interact with your writing and the sum will be all the richer."
- David Brin

Y ou have your tools together, and now you must write. You are going to learn my favorite tools to pen a banger, my take on the famous hero's journey, and more. But before we go there, I want to introduce a new road to writing your novel.

Take some time to think about the most interesting people in your life. Think about the way their eyes are shaped, and how they look at you or avoid eye contact all together. What is their ethnicity? What is the tone of their complexion? Are there any visible marks or tattoos on their bodies? Are there any tattoos that are not visible on their bodies?

How do they dress? Do they fashion the labels or do they prefer to shop for less? How do they wear their hair? How bright is their smile? What kinds of food do they enjoy? What irritates them? What brings them joy? If you are intimate with them how do they smell? How does their skin feel against yours? What does their body look like naked? Do they seem ashamed or confident when naked?

Do they pass gas? If so what does it smell like? Does a certain food cause them to have to go to the bathroom? If so, do they close the door or leave it open? Do they cry easily? Where were they raised? What kind of mother do they have? What about their father? Does their breath stink? If so, are you ashamed to tell them? If so why? How do you think they will react?

If I irritated you by these questions, if you've been in my presence think about me. How do I wear my hair for the moment? How are my eyes shaped? Are they large or small? Do they hold mystery or do they tell you everything about me immediately? What about my breasts? Do they look real or fake? Do they appear soft or hard? Are my lips large? Are they pink? If you've been in my presence, do I yell a lot? If so do I make you nervous? If so why? Do I appear confident or weak? Do you get the picture? If not, why?

Characters are the reason we watch our favorite shows or wait in line to see great movies. Yet for some reason, we choose to treat characters as if they are an afterthought when we develop our stories. This is a disaster waiting to happen. If you want to write a best seller, and I know you do, you need to create characters that last long after your book is closed.

I know some of you were embarrassed when I asked the questions about passing gas, or using the bathroom. But what was the feeling that resonated with you when I asked the questions? Remember those feelings clearly! Because this is what it takes to make a great book. You have to be willing to talk about things that people don't want to discuss. You have to be brave enough to scratch up emotions, and be not so politically correct.

THE END. PART 1

People bore easily and the way to excite them is by honesty. Sometimes brutal honesty.

When I wrote *Raunchy*, I had enough of books on the market that did nothing to rouse my emotions. I dared to write about a woman so horrid, that the mere mentioning of her name would disgust my readers for years to come. I wanted the character to be so real, if my fans had a baby girl, Harmony would be the last name they'd call her. And if you talk to my fans, I'm positive I've achieved this result.

You need to move into the heart of your story to captivate, and the way you do that is by making your readers *feel something*. You want them to be mad, angry, disgusted, sad, happy, inspired and you even want them to laugh. Developing strong characters is the *only* way to do this.

If you disagree, consider for a moment how boring it would be to watch a movie about cars with no drivers, a home with no family, a football game with no players, or a relationship with no lovers. No characters equal no life experiences and that truly is the bottom line.

Let's answer a couple of the questions we talked about earlier. Think about a character you are considering creating. Don't worry about knowing them completely, because as your story goes along, their traits will evolve and so will your storyline. What you are doing is laying the groundwork for who your characters are, in the hopes of finding out who they will be. Your characters will evolve with your book and when who they are is finally revealed, that's when the magic begins!

1st, **How does your main character look?**
> What color is his or her hair?
> Eyes?
> What ethnicity are they?

-40-

2nd **How do they talk?**

: This is especially important when you consider that each character in your story, will speak differently in dialogue. When writing dialogue between your characters, the difference should be evident. Someone from Harvard may not speak the same as someone who didn't graduate from high school. (Unless you purposely write it that way.)

3rd **What kinds of clothes do they wear?**

Do they look good in their clothes?

Are there clothes clean or dirty?

Are they designer or inexpensive?

Are they handmade?

4th **What kind of personality do they have?**

Are they nice?

Are they rude or mean?

If so why?

What kind of personality does their mother have?

What about the father?

What irritates them?

What delights them?

What kind of people do they choose to associate with?

What kind of people are they attracted to?

These are the things you need to think thoroughly through when you're selecting your leading man or woman. Why? Because the way to leave a lasting impression is through your characters.

THE END. PART 1

Now, grab your Character Sheet and think of your main character. Write your responses here:

Character Name: (Do not select a name that is traditional.)

_____

_____

Age:

_____

Hair:

_____

Height:

_____

Weight:

_____

Job:

_____

Weaknesses:

_____

Strengths:

_____

Relationship Status:

_____

_____

Notes:

_____

_____

_____

_____

_____

_____

_____

_____

_____

_____

_____

_____

_____

_____

_____

_____

_____

_____

_____

_____

CHAPTER FIVE

Developing Your Plot Through My Take On The Hero's Journey

"If you believe you can make a living as a writer, you already have enough ego."
- David Brin

I'm not going to use a bunch of terms that will confuse you. Why? Because throughout my career, I never had an agent, or publisher ask me if I knew how to apply a bunch of fancy terms. At the end of the day they wanted to know what my book was about and they were concerned with whether or not it was good or bad. Anything else, in my opinion, and theirs, was trivial.

Not only am I going to throw out all the rules of writing, I'm going to tell you to throw away the outline too. I never started with an outline. If I had, I doubt that I would have as many books written as I do. Outlines can ruin a project I've seen it. You'll force yourself to think of every moment before it happens, and by the time you write your book, you are totally exhausted. I think you should know about your characters, locations and the ending of your book, but that's about it, my friend. Don't worry, we'll talk about endings later.

Now am I totally against outlines? No! I just don't want you to bother with them in the beginning. If you disagree with me, and you believe outlines are so great and that they work brilliantly, why are you reading this book?

I'm not trying to be crass, but I want you to think for a moment what I am *really* saying. If your method works so great, why not stick to it? Outlines slow down creativity. In my opinion, a wordy synopsis does too. Although, most times before I start my novel I can tell you in three sentences what my book is about, but that is the extent of it. In the beginning you are not to do anything that will slow you down including writing a long ass outline.

Instead I want you to do the unthinkable. I want you to throw caution to the wind and simply write. But…and here is where I might confuse you a little, when you finish your first draft, and its time for rewrites, I want you to consider the Hero's Journey.

What is the Hero's Journey?
The Hero's Journey is a pattern identified by the American Scholar Joseph Campbell. It describes the adventure of the archetype known as the hero. It is meant to give you a formula, and a blueprint, to make an exciting fiction story. If you follow it as closely as possible, your book should be adventurous and fun. To make it easier to understand, using our story *Bad Pop Bad Cop*, I'm going to lead you through the formula. However, to learn about the complete process, feel free to Google the topic and read away.

T. Styles' Take On The Hero's Journey
DEPARTURE
1. **The Call To Adventure**: Is the point in the hero's (protagonist) life, when they are called to do something great or majorly different.
2. **Refusal Of The Call**: Is the point in the story where the hero refuses to change or listen to the call.

3. <u>**Super Natural Aid**</u>: When the hero finally answers the call, he or she is given an aid to help with the journey.
4. <u>**The Crossing Of The First Threshold**</u>: This is when the hero has become involved in the adventure and leaves his or her world as they know it. Things become dangerous, and the rules are unknown.
5. <u>**The Belly Of The Whale**</u>: This step represents the final separation from the hero's world. It is also referred to as the lowest point in the hero's life. Something dark, and unknown must occur at this point in the story.

INITIATION

6. <u>**The Road Of Trials**</u>: Is a series of trials and tasks that the hero must go through in order to transform.
7. <u>**The Meeting With The Goddess**</u>: This is the point in the story where the person experiences love. Unconditional love. Can be experienced by someone or can be the love within.
8. <u>**Woman As A Temptress**</u>: This is the point in the story where the hero may stray from his/her quest. It could be because of earthly temptations. It doesn't have to be a woman who tempts, just as long as the hero is tempted in some way.
9. <u>**Atonement With The Father**</u>: This point in the story where the hero must be confronted by whom or whatever holds the ultimate power in his life. This is the center point of the story. Although it may be described as a male entity, it doesn't have to be male. Just someone or something with incredible power in the hero's life. In

the journey the hero must be killed spiritually, so that the new self can be born.

10. **Apotheosis**: In real life when someone dies, the spirit moves to a place of divine knowledge, love, compassion and bliss. This is a God-like state. So must be the same with your character at this point in your story. They must come into a point of divine knowledge. It's almost like a state of peace or fulfillment.

11. **The Ultimate Boon**: Is when the hero achieves his or her goal. All the previous steps in the journey are getting the hero prepared for this moment.

RETURN

12. **Refusal Of The Return**: Is the point where the hero refuses to go back to his or her old life.

13. **The Magic Flight**: Sometimes, not all the time, the hero must return home with something that the jealous Gods or villains have been hiding.

14. **Rescue From The Flight**: Just as the hero needs a guide to start the quest (Supernatural Aid), sometimes he or she may need an aid to return them home to everyday life.

15. **The Crossing Of The Return Threshold**: In order to return, and return without disregard to the new person the hero has become, he or she must return with the wisdom they have learned. The wisdom learned and obtained must be translated in the past life.

16. **Master Of The Two Worlds**: It means effectively achieving the balance between the old world and the new world.

THE END. PART 1

17. **Freedom To Live**: This step leads to the freedom of fear. You are neither regretting the past nor reveling in the future. You are at peace.

Making Sense Of The Journey

Okay, now that you have a brief understanding of the Hero's Journey, lets apply the following scenario to what we learned above.

Consider our book, *Bad Pop Bad Cop*. In this book the plot is as follows. A father, whose name is Todd, has an argument with his eldest daughter, her name is Tiffany, in their home one night. The mother, her name is Linda, and their youngest daughter Shelly, are also in the house but stay out of the argument. Although they say nothing, they are tired of Todd's drunken behavior towards his family.

The next morning, when Shelly awakens, she discovers that Tiffany was raped and murdered. Because the father has had drunken violent episodes in the past, he is immediately taken into custody because of the fight the night before. At first, no one disputes the arrest.

Based on what we know about the scenario above, we can assume the following using the Hero's Journey:

DEPARTURE

1. **The Call To Adventure** – In our scenario, Shelly discovers by mistake that even though her father Todd was taken into custody for the murder and rape, that her uncle Mark, who is also a decorated officer, may have been involved in the crime. Shelly immediately brings it to her mother's attention, but because of fear, her mother refuses to do anything. Upon speaking to her best friend Nikki who lives across the street, she advises Shelly to tell the police. The call to adventure is Nikki's request that Shelly alert the authorities.

2. **Refusal Of The Call** – Instead of going to the cops, Shelly refuses because she's afraid that she may be wrong, and that she may be forced to testify against her uncle, whom she loves. Shelly has refused the call.

3. **Supernatural Aid** – Instead of supporting Shelly in her decision to remain silent, Nikki doesn't let the matter go. Instead when Nikki is asked to check the camera that records the front of her house by her parents, after their car is vandalized, she discovers video footage of Mark leaving Shelly's house in his police cruiser the night of the crime. She snaps a few pictures of the scene and shows them to Shelly. Nikki vows to help her anyway she can. Nikki is Shelly's supernatural aid.

4. **The Crossing Of The First Threshold** – Upon seeing the proof, Shelly calls Mark and asks him was he at their home the night of the crime. He doesn't seem forthcoming, and asks why she wants to know. When she explains his car was seen leaving the crime, and that she has pictures, he demands that she keep the evidence to herself, and to remain put. He says he's on his way over. For the first time in her life, she refuses and he threatens to kill her and her mother. Trying to keep her mother safe, she runs away from home with Nikki, and they stay in a hotel until they can sort things out.

Shelly crossed the threshold when she advised Mark that she was aware of his crime. Even if she wanted to stay out of the matter, she cannot from this point on.

5. **The Belly Of The Whale**- After some time, Shelly and Nikki learn more about Mark and his unsavory ways. They discover that he is a bad cop on the take, who like her father, is also an alcoholic. When Shelly calls her mother to let her know what she is dealing with, she discovers that she has been murdered, probably by Mark. Remorseful, and saddened by the loss of her mother, she understands she can never go back to life as she knows it.

INITIATION

1. **The Road Of Trials** – Although Shelly is devastated by the loss of her mother, she is determined more than ever to win her father's freedom. In the midst of the drama, Mark finds out where the girls are hiding and places bounties on their heads for $50,000. They try to throw Mark and his hit men off by staying low, when one day Shelly is struck by a car resulting in a broken arm.

Madeline, a whore, sees the entire incident take place. After Nikki pleads with her to help her friend, Madeline helps them get medical attention and hides them so that Mark doesn't know their whereabouts. Madeline knows first hand the kind of man Mark is because he rapes her and steals her money at least once a month.

Shelly eventually recuperates and doesn't give up on solving the case. Instead she is more determined than ever to bring Mark to justice. She also meets a young man named Chance, who seems to be smitten by her.

2. **The Meeting With The Goddess** – Shelly learns that instead of being weak, she's actually very strong. She has a dream where her mother comes to her, and tells her that everything will be okay. This dream comes right when she needs it because prior to the revelation, she was lost and for a brief moment, on the verge of giving up. She also gravitates more to her new love interest, Chance.

3. **Woman As A Temptress** – After some time Shelly strays away from the quest to bring Mark to justice. She'd rather spend more time with her boyfriend. Besides, Chance promises to take her away from it all, and she actually considers it because he has a good job in construction. Besides, Mark almost killed her and she is tired of being scared for her life and her boyfriend's. She wonders what it would be like to finally worry about herself, and not

her family.

4. **Atonement With The Father** – This is the center point of the story. Shelly decides to go to the media and tell them about her uncle and his possible involvement in the murder of her sister. The media goes wild and her name is on the front page of every paper across America. Mark is now under heavy scrutiny. She speaks with her father and tells him that she loves him and although she believes he is innocent, she is fighting this battle in her sister's name, not his. She speaks about the regret she feels for how he treated her as a child, and says that although she was angry, she forgives him.

5. **Apotheosis** – In love and stronger than ever, Shelly feels powerful. She's no longer scared and is willing to do whatever she can to defend her sister's honor.

6. **The Ultimate Boon** – When Mark traps Shelly, Nikki and Chance in an alley, he murders Nikki. Chance charges Mark and is beaten unmercifully. Just when the battle is almost over, and Mark is prepared to pull the trigger, Shelly rushes him, knocks the gun out of his hand and shoots Mark instead. Mark is killed instantly. The achievement of the goal is done and complete.

RETURN
1. **Refusal Of The Return** – Although she won the battle, and Todd is released from prison, Shelly doesn't want to return home. The media declares her a hero and all she can think about is the loss of her sister, mother and best friend.

Chance tries his best to convince her to return, advising that she needs to be reunited with her father, but she refuses. Chance doesn't want to drop the issue because without Todd, Shelly seems so lonely. Especially considering the murder of her loved ones.

2. **The Magic Flight** - If the Boon is physical, the hero may have to escape with it. In our scenario it isn't so we can disregard this step. Just keep this step in mind if you have a boon which can be returned. A boon is something helpful or physical. It could have been the pictures that Nikki discovered of Mark fleeing the scene on the video footage outside of her home.

3. **Rescue From Without** - Often there may be other aids to bring heroes back home. Since Shelly doesn't want to return, in our story, Chance gives her a drink laced with a sleeping pill and she falls to sleep. When she awakens, she is home and she is temporarily angry until she sees her father's face. He hugs her and tells her how much he needs her, and she cries. She feels safe and is no longer mad at her lover.

4. **The Crossing Of The Return Threshold** – Shelly becomes familiar with life back home without her mother, sister and best friend. She and Chance get an apartment in the area and she learns how to love her father again.

5. **Master Of Two Worlds** – Shelly is home, she is comfortable with her new life and she is no longer afraid to live alone with Chance and to start anew. She keeps all the strength she attained on her journey to live a purposeful life.

6. **Freedom To Live** – Shelly lives in the moment with her boyfriend and no longer in the past. She finally lives happily ever after. Or not, if you're like me and love sequels.

Using Google, research more on the Hero's Journey.

THE END. PART 1

Record what you've learned here:

_____

_____

_____

_____

_____

_____

_____

_____

_____

_____

_____

Now using what you know, when its time to do your rewrites, how will you apply it to your story? Use the worksheet following this chapter to answer the question.

Your Hero's Journey Worksheet
(Use For Rewrites Only)

DEPARTURE
1. <u>The Call To Adventure</u>

_____

_____

_____

_____

_____

_____

_____

_____

2. <u>Refusal of the Call</u>

_____

_____

_____

_____

_____

_____

_____

_____

3. <u>Supernatural Aid</u>

_____

_____

_____

_____

_____

_____

_____

_____

THE END. PART 1

4. **<u>The Crossing of The First Threshold</u>**

_____
_____
_____
_____
_____
_____
_____
_____
_____

5. **<u>The Belly of The Whale</u>**

_____
_____
_____
_____
_____
_____
_____
_____
_____

INITIATION
1. **<u>The Road of Trials</u>**

_____
_____
_____
_____
_____
_____
_____
_____
_____

2. **The Meeting With the Goddess**

_____

_____

_____

_____

_____

_____

_____

_____

_____

3. **Woman as a Temptress**

_____

_____

_____

_____

_____

_____

_____

_____

4. **Atonement with the Father**

_____

_____

_____

_____

_____

THE END. PART 1

5. <u>**Apotheosis**</u>

_____

6. <u>**The Ultimate Boon**</u>

_____

<u>**RETURN**</u>

1. <u>**Refusal of the Return**</u>

_____

2. **The Magic Flight**

3. **Rescue From Without**

4. **The Crossing of the Return Threshold**

5. **Master of Two Worlds**

THE END. PART 1

_____

6. **<u>Freedom to Live</u>**

_____

CHAPTER SIX
Things You Must ALWAYS Consider

"Why shouldn't truth be stranger than fiction? Fiction, after all, has to make sense."
- Mark Twain

Okay, we are almost ready! I know you think you needed more to form your book, but trust me it's almost time. I have included a daily passage in this book that you need to read the start of writing each day. I believe hands on is the best way to learn, but first I need to discus the items below. You're not going to remember them all. In fact, you may not remember any of them. But over the course of your career, as you return to this book to write another, you should always start here. Before long these points will be engrained in your memory like your address or phone number.

1. **TAKE TWO MINUTES TO THINK OF A SCENE BEFORE YOU WRITE IT**
   I know I just told you to write to your heart's content. And I sincerely want you to do so. However, you should give yourself at least two minutes to think of a scene before you write it. Think of it as an athlete stretching before he begins his sport. You might find that you go a total different route once you start, but at least you have direction. I don't

want you to write down your ideas. During the thirty days the pen should not touch your book until you are ready to write. Just think about your scene and when you're ready…GO!

2. **WRITE FIVE PAGES A DAY**
Even if it's a page full of dialogue, I expect you to write no less than five pages a day. If you write large, I expect you to push out seven. You can achieve your daily goals in many ways.

If you are at work, you can keep your notebook with you and write on your breaks. If you are worried about people bothering you at lunch, write in your car. If you don't own a vehicle, you can write on the way to work on the bus or train. When you come home, since you have had the conversation with your CFF's, you are to write at your scheduled time.

Get my point? You are to be religious with this process. Excuses, I find, are reasons we give ourselves to quit so that we don't have to attain our goals. We are not allowing our minds to hold us back any longer. You will get that book out, and you will do it now.

Although you are to free style, try to cram the below items within the first five pages of your book.

a. **A hook**
- You want a sentence that will grab your reader immediately. The hook should be the first two sentences.

b. **Introduction of your protagonist**

c. **Introduction of the protagonist's main problem**
d. **Establishment of the setting
   and genre** (Sci-fi, urban fiction,
   etc.)
e. **The tone of the story**

The first pages hook your readers, publishers and maybe even editors. This absolutely is one of the reasons that some writers despise the first five. But it's absolutely necessary to hit them hard in the beginning or you will lose them to another book. Don't waste your time on giving too much background. You must seduce right away!

There are millions of books on the market. Millions! You have to persuade a reader to stay with you. By purchasing your book, you are essentially asking, *"Will you stay with me for the next 7 to 10 hours?"* If you don't hit them and keep them, the answer will be, *"Get the fuck out of my face! Your book was some trash!"*

When I wrote *Black & Ugly*, about a young lady who was beautiful but hated her dark skin, the first line was, *"I knew I was ugly the moment my mother gave me a mirror."* Immediately you are given the tone of the story and you are hooked.

You can also hook a reader using epigraphs. In my novel *Raunchy*, the epigraph leading into the story reads, *"Why should my life change just 'cause I got kids? Shit...I brought them in this world...what more do they want?"*

Times have changed and so must we. People have so many avenues and so many ways to be entertained. There are movies, the Internet and great social networking sites. You also have popular reality TV shows like *The Real Housewives of Atlanta*, which is favored because of the drama and confrontational scenes. You must do the same with your books. Create chaos!

3. **NO REWRITING FOR THE FIRST 30 DAYS**
You can't finish this book in 30 days if you rewrite. The only thing you should bother yourself with in the beginning are the basics. What are the basics? Your characters and their quirks.

Beyond that, I don't want you to do anything but write. If you are using your computer, I don't even want you checking for spelling and format. If you're using shorthand, and have bad writing, as long as you can understand your words move on. You have a deadline to meet, which cannot be achieved if you tend to things you will change anyway during the rewrite process.

4. **MOVE PAST EXTENSIVE DESCRIPTIONS**
For your rough draft you are not to busy yourself with elaborate descriptions that may stunt your flow. For example, if you want to describe a house, and it does not have a SERIOUS impediment on the story, use a Placer instead. Ex. *The house was beautiful. It had **(Describe house here)**. We marveled at the design and figured one day we would live in such a place if we hustled and hustled hard.*

By using the placer: (**Describe house here)**, during the rewrite process, you can get as detailed as necessary. If you are one of the lucky few whom are not stunted by descriptions, feel free to avoid the placers and describe away! However, if you are anything like me, getting too far in depth can slow you down.

Also, make sure you don't waste time describing non-essential characters in detail. Unless a character is key to the story, it is quite all right to give them bland titles. For instance, *'the cute white nurse'* or *'the handsome black police officer'*. Not only are you freeing up some of your creative energy, you are also allowing the readers to envision the character as he or she chooses.

5. **IF IT SOUNDS STUPID, WRITE IT ANYWAY**
I can't count the number of times, someone will bring me a great idea and say, *"But it sounds stupid right?"* The whole time I'm thinking, *"Are you kidding? It's great!"*

Please don't double think your thoughts or ideas, especially during the first 30 days. If you feel like it's stupid, or might not make any sense, that's where the magic begins. When I wrote the novel *Shyt List*, I thought it would be massively stupid to give my main character Yvonna Harris, a mental disorder. I figured in the street literature market, in which I write, my readers might not welcome this trait. They wanted fast paced novels with drugs, guns and money. Boy was I wrong.

This one small move has allowed me to be able to write fulltime. To date *Shyt List* is the most popular book on my publishing label, *The Cartel Publications*. I haven't looked back since. I hate to think what would have become of my career, had I thwarted my own success by leaving out what I felt was stupid. Feeling uncomfortable means you are moving out of your comfort zone.

Always avoid the idea you are most likely to write because it is popular. For instance, giving a character the name Jill, or a man the name James.

Look for names that aren't common. In *Shyt List*, my character Ming has a son named *Boy* and fans love it. Rid yourself of the normalcy and jump on the wild side. Embrace your crazy ideas because chances are, you're on to something new and original!

6. **USE ALL OF YOUR SENSES**
    Many books do not come to life because the writer fails to pull you in. One of the ways you do this is by using the five senses throughout your book.
    Examples:
    1. (**Sight**) Shelly saw the bright orange flecks of the sun as she lie on her back.
    2. (**Hearing**) Shelly heard the soft sounds of the tires rolling over gravel in the distance.
    3. (**Touch**) Shelly could feel the cool blades of grass under her fingertips.
    4. (**Smell**) The scent of the earth after the recent rain was pleasing to Shelly's nose.
    5. (**Taste**) Shelly pulled a blade of grass from the earth, and sat it on the tip of her tongue. She could taste the dew's sweetness.

The key is to use as many of your senses as possible to form your story. We have our senses to experience the world around us. Do not cheat your readers by failing to paint the perfect picture. Using senses properly, will force your readers into your story where you'll keep them for the long run.

7. **NEVER JUDGE YOUR CHARACTERS**

When I first started writing, I did an amazing job of judging my characters. I would convince myself that the reason I judged them, was to show the world how life really should be. I was out of line and didn't have a psychology degree. The nerve!

First off at the time I judged my characters, I didn't have the best relationships with my mother, son and other family members. Hell, I still have some screwed up relationships lingering around. Back then however, I was mad at the world because I felt I'd been given the shit end of the stick in a few places in my life. I couldn't see beauty through the darkness until later in life. I was, by all accounts, human. Yet I would point fingers in my characters faces and shaped the way they interacted with one another, when often they clearly wanted to perform in a different way.

When I wrote *Raunchy*, a story about an alcoholic abusive mother, I stopped playing games. I wrote the book I wanted to read with the emotions I wanted to stir up in my readers. If Harmony Phillips wanted to sit on a toilet, and scratch her vagina raw due to all of the diseases she contracted because of having unprotected sex, I allowed her to do just that. To date, it is one of my most acclaimed novels.

Never judge your characters, allow them to be who they are. People will respect this quality, and your fan base will grow.

8. DON'T DESCRIBE CHARACTER'S CLOTHING TRADITIONALLY

There's nothing worse than a writer describing a character's clothing, as if they were speaking of inventory. You want to make their clothing a part of the story. For instance, never write, *"She was wearing a black leather jacket, and a red mini skirt as she walked through the room."* Instead write, *"She tugged nervously on her black leather jacket. Her red mini skirt clung to her thick thighs and it looked as if it were painted on her body."*

This will take some getting use to because until late, it took me a while to fully understand how important this method was to build engaging storylines. But now that I have this jewel, I will never let it go.

9. SHOW DON'T TELL

This has to be the single most important reason books flop. Writers refuse to challenge themselves by showing the reader versus telling them what is going on in a story.

We are in the age of the movies. In the early 19th century writers could tell readers what was going on to their heart's content. Movies, TV's and the like were not as prevalent. Now if a writer wants to get in this game to win, she has to show and prove. Literally. Telling is giving narration. It doesn't have specific characters or scenes. It's second hand information. Similar to if I walked up to you and said, *"So and so said your feet stink and they looked disgusted when they said it too."*

Now if you saw it yourself, and you noticed the way so and so's face squinted as he discussed your feet, and if you saw the way I held my stomach and balled over in laughter, and it was described to the reader in vivid detail, then it is showing.

Consider this sentence:

Chance walked nervously to Shelly in an effort to get her attention.

The sentence is not bad, but it is boring. Let's try this instead:

Chance trudged slowly toward Shelly. His palms were filled with puddles of sweat and his temples throbbed due to nervousness.

You want to paint the picture for the reader. Be considerate of their time and attention. They chose your book so don't let them feel as if they made a mistake.

10. MAKE DIALOGUE REAL

Although the first 30 days are not for rewriting, I do want you to speak your dialogue scenes out loud. The reason? You want it to be realistic. Often what you think looks good on paper, sounds dry, corny or unrealistic when read aloud. If you read it before you publish it, you can save your readers from a boring experience. Take a few minutes as you go along to make your dialogue right! It will be well worth it.

11. GIVE CHARACTERS SEPARATE AGENDAS

This is a major jewel so take heed. To make the most out of your book, give everybody in a scene a different agenda. It doesn't make a difference if they're friends or not. You want to make it confrontational at every cost. If there are two friends in the car, and one wants to go to McDonald's, for the sake of drama make the other want to go to Burger

King *and* be vocal about it. This is a must have jewel for writers and should not be ignored.

12. CRAM AS MANY CONFLICTS IN YOUR STORY AS POSSIBLE

Tying in to what we were saying above, you want to also add many confrontational scenes to your storyline. Even if they don't make any sense to other scenes written. Why? Because if you write as many dramatic scenes as possible, you will begin to learn more about your characters and eliminate boredom.

The worse case scenario, if you find after rewrites that a scene does not apply to your storyline, you can always take it out, and use it for future novels. Saving deleted scenes means there will never be a scene gone to waste.

13. KNOW YOUR VIEW

Although in street fiction, we have been known to mix the first person voice with the third, you must be careful if you are looking to solicit your work to major publishing houses. This is often frowned upon and can come across as amateur.

In *Raunchy*, I reserved the right to use both. Keep in mind I self-published my own novel. The majority of the book was written in first person. However, when reflecting, I wrote in third person. The *Library Journal* has since recognized this book but it was a risky move. This only worked because it was clear to the reader when I was in reflection and when I was using first person.

Also, some writers get confused on what can be known when writing in certain voices. In the below sentence, Shelly is longing for her boyfriend Chance's touch. But can you tell me what is wrong?

"I was in love, and I needed to kiss his lips. Without asking, I pulled him close to me and his heart rate sped up. He was anticipating what I would do next and he wanted me so badly, he was minutes away from passing out due to anticipation."

For starters, everything is wrong with that passage. Shelly is awfully presumptuous to know how fast his heart rate sped up and that he wanted to pass out due to wanting her so badly. In first person, she is not privy to the internal body mechanics of other characters. This is why you should definitely consider which voice you select before you write your book. There are benefits and negatives to both.

First Person

1. First person is the most natural voice to use, probably because we use this voice in everyday life. The author is essentially the narrator and must inject personality so that readers are involved immediately.

2. Whenever the character speaks of himself, you must remember to use "I".

3. You cannot tell someone something that happened to somebody else internally. As a result, perspectives are limited. In other words, if I'm using first person, I do not know the status of every character's bodily functions nor do I know what they are thinking, unless they tell me.

4. If done well, the first person voice will give the reader logic and motivations to

characters that might otherwise seem evil or immoral.

Third Person
1. Third person can be more objective and less emotional.
2. The author is free to cover all characters without bias toward any one character.
3. The author can be omniscient which is what most authors truly want. Omniscient means all knowing. So like in our example above, with Shelly, if it were written in third person, the author would be free to describe what each character is feeling inside or thinking.

However, the writer should steer clear from going into depth about every character.

There are many more advantages and disadvantages to both. Using the resources available in this book, be sure to research which voice is best before writing your novel.

14. KNOW YOUR ENDING EVEN IF IT CHANGES
Although I don't want you to mull over knowing your ending too much in the beginning, but if you can without getting turned around, please take advantage of this jewel. Why? Because if you know your ending, everything you write before then will lead up to that moment.

Here's the thing…knowing your ending doesn't mean knowing every detail. When I ask you to know your ending, I'm asking for the basics. In the end of our novel with Shelly and her uncle who is a corrupted cop, we know that she will have a face off with him in an alley with her friends, and murder him. That's the ending. It's simple and to the point, and all of our scenes before the ending should be leading up to that moment.

15. LEAVE EACH CHAPTER WITH A CLIFF-HANGER

Lets face it; people claim they hate to be left hanging. However, readers don't know what they want. Think about any amusement park your mind can imagine. Lines are always around the corner because people love suspense. Even if they know inevitably that the ride will come to an end, part of their psyche can't say for sure they'll make it off the ride alive.

You never, ever, take the reader where they want to go. And you never, ever, leave your chapter giving them the conclusions they need. You leave them hanging…always, and that my friends, is how you make a page-turner!

16. GIVE YOUR MAIN CHARACTER CATCH PHRASES & HOBBIES

By giving your characters catch phrases, you engage readers. I will often repeat a catch phrase on my Facebook account from one of my novels, and because the characters are well developed, the readers always respond. Because they know without me even saying the character's name or book, who I'm talking about. And everyone else, who didn't read the book, will feel left out. For instance, in the book *Raunchy*, the character Kali, would always say, "*I got you.*" Whenever he said this it usually meant murder was on the horizon. When I would put the phrase on my page, fans would respond and we would go back and forth.

Also, give your characters hobbies. Try to avoid simple hobbies like reading, or writing unless it goes deeper. Use hobbies like candle making, scrapbooking, quilting, gardening, etc. Don't just say the character has a hobby, show the hobby within your storyline. Of course you might have to research the hobby to make it realistic, but that is your duty as an author.

17. WORK WITH MULTIPLE OUTCOMES TO THROW READERS OFF

Let's say one character is the frontrunner to commit a certain crime. You should raise suspicion with at least two other characters in your book, to throw readers off. With suspicion heightened on the other two, you soften it on your frontrunner, the person actually guilty. When the suspect is finally revealed, the reader will be blown away.

18. **STOP WITH THE PERFECTION ALREADY**

I'm going to give it to you straight; readers hate perfect families, faces, people and lives. There's nothing more sickening than everybody in a book looking like money or a model. Having the best clothing, the best boyfriend, the best friends, the best car, the best job, etc. Take a walk on the wild side. Make your leading character unattractive, or an unsavory individual. There are enough books on the market about the fairy princess. Don't add to this unrealistic perception because the bottom line is, these types of people don't exist.

Notes:

_____
_____
_____
_____
_____
_____
_____
_____
_____
_____
_____
_____
_____
_____
_____
_____
_____
_____
_____
_____
_____
_____
_____
_____
_____
_____
_____

CHAPTER SEVEN
The 30-Day Countdown

Hint: Please write your name in the blank spaces on the page before you read the passage.

DAY 1

"Those rituals of getting ready to write produce a kind of trance state."
- John Barth

You're ready! You're amped! It's contagious! Don't you just love it when you have a plan, _____? Don't let anybody get in your way, including yourself. You have a mission. And if you choose to accept, it means you MUST write five pages a day. You'll find it easier to write today, especially if you attended my seminar because your first five are all ready to go! Feed off of this steam and milk it for all it's worth.

If you haven't attended my seminar, don't forget that your first sentence must demand that the reader give you their undivided attention! You only get one chance to make a first impression. Consider the tone and what you want to convey. Are you embracing the reader in drama? Did you start with a little mystery, in the hopes of luring them for the long hall? This is the time to do it. Right now! You won't get a better chance to prove what kind of writer you are. So lets make it count.

Since you've already enrolled in my forum, so that you can connect with other writers, please check in today to introduce yourself. The link is below:

http://groups.yahoo.com/group/theendnovelin30days/

Please don't take this step as trivial. I find that it's much easier to accomplish a task, when I have a great support system. Even now in my career, I rely on the support of my peers to push me to the next level.

Also remember to take a few moments before you write to think about your scenes. This doesn't have to be written down. The purpose of this tool is to exercise your

THE END. PART 1

mind at the start of each day. You'll jog your creative juices and also you'll have a general direction to move in.

Creative Exercise For The Day

Do you keep a journal? If not why?

_____
_____
_____
_____

If so can you draw from some of your personal experiences to spark your storyline?

_____
_____
_____
_____

Notes:

_____
_____
_____
_____
_____
_____
_____
_____
_____
_____
_____

DAY 2

"A lot of people talk about writing. The secret is to write, not talk."
- Jackie Collins

I'm proud of you, _____. You are back and eager to put your foot down and fulfill your dreams. As you plow into your second day, I'm reminded about when I first started writing. It was a book that I never want to read again in life, titled *Rainbow Heart*.

I remember pouring my heart into that novel. When it was complete, I mulled over it again and again. It was important for me to get each paragraph perfect before moving to the next.

I described the way the sun shined. How it felt against the main character's skin. Every detail in the tiny apartment the story was based out of, was explained with such clarity, you'd forget it was in the projects. I described every song played on the radio, the way children laughed and their teeth blinged. At one point I believe I even described the ingredients necessary to make a full meal! The details in my book would've been fine if someone was looking to buy the apartment and the characters to cook their meals too. For a reader looking to simply enjoy a book, it was inconsiderate and drab.

At the end of the day, I wrote all of that foolishness and forgot two things. One to have fun and two, to just write a damn book! I was so concerned with constructing a story that I forgot to put my heart into it.

Rainbow Heart took the longest for me to write, a little over a year, and it was also the most unsuccessful book of my career. Don't make the same mistake I did. I truly believe you can study long and wrong.

THE END. PART 1

I ask as you start your project today that you have fun, and simply write!

Creative Exercise For The Day

Who was the most interesting person that you've run into today? And why?

_____
_____
_____
_____

How does this person make you feel?

_____
_____
_____
_____

What did you talk about?

_____
_____
_____
_____

Do you want to speak with them again? If so, why?

_____
_____
_____
_____

DAY 3

"Don't get it right, just get it written."
- James Thurber

By now you know the importance of getting 'er done. At this point you should have ten pages of great, uninhibited, free-styled work in your possession. You aren't concerning yourself with misspelled words, or formats. Are you, _____? Your only concern is knowing your characters and letting them speak honestly to you while you try your hardest to consider the jewels we talked about along the way.

Remember to take advantage of any free time you have to get a few sentences out. Not everyone can steal a couple of hours a night. However, this does not give you a pass to not write your five pages.

When I wrote my fourth book, I was a representative at a cell phone store. It was one of the most profitable stores in the market and the most profitable store in the company. I stayed busy with very little time to steal moments to write. However, when I had my breaks, I would write in the bathroom. Yes I did say the bathroom. I would write on my fifteen-minute breaks and my entire lunch period. I had a sandwich in one hand and my pen in the other because I was determined to make a career as a writer.

If you have to pull your car over before you come home and sit in a parking lot, get it done. If you have to go to the library, before you go home, get it done. If you have to sit in the closet that has a light, get it done. Make no more excuses, they truly are dead and old.

In order to be successful, you must have the same unwavering desire to finish what you start.

THE END. PART 1

Creative Exercise For The Day

What major obstacle is hindering your process?

_____

_____

_____

What steps can you take to avoid this hindrance in the future?

_____

_____

_____

Thinking ahead, what places can you consider to write at in the future?

_____

_____

_____

Notes:

_____

_____

_____

_____

_____

DAY 4

"The discipline of the writer is to learn to be still and listen to what the subject has to tell him."
- Rachel Carson

I remember when I first thought of the character Evelyn from my first book *Rainbow Heart*. I wanted so badly to write a good story. One that my mother, sister and friends would be proud of. At that point, I knew that everyone would read my book in an attempt to get a glimpse of my life, especially considering the novel was a lesbian tale. I knew if nothing else, nosiness would not keep them away from the book as they asked themselves, *'Is Toy talking about herself?'*

In the course of developing my character, I remembered holding Evelyn back. When she wanted to say one thing, I would clean her up and make her say another. I absolutely had everything to do with the dryness of my first book. It would've been so much better had I allowed my characters to just be. If I had allowed them to say what they wanted to say to one another.

Readers respect honesty in life and they love it in books too. It is your job to center yourself when you write, and consider who your characters are,_____.
Let them live their lives, and you stay out of it. If you want to control a life, control your own by finishing what you start, starting with this book. By keeping this in mind always, the results will be lasting.

Creative Exercise For The Day

What is your character saying to you today?

_____

_____

THE END. PART 1

_____
_____

Does it make you uncomfortable? And if so why?

_____
_____
_____
_____

How do you think your family will feel about your novel?

_____
_____
_____
_____

If they respond negatively do you think you will care?

_____
_____
_____
_____

Notes:

_____
_____
_____
_____
_____
_____
_____

DAY 5

"The most beautiful stories always start with wreckage."
- Jack London

In *Raunchy*, I wrote a story about Harmony Phillips. Her grandmother and uncle sexually abused her. To make matters worse, her mother first introduced her to alcohol. The novel is graphic, raw and honest. Although there was a method to my madness, it was not my job to necessarily explain what it was during my writing process. I am a storyteller, and I accept this job with pride. At the end of the day, if you remember nothing else remember this, you must not be afraid to write stories that appear to be train wrecks waiting to happen.

I took no pleasure when I wrote the scene in which Harmony Phillips was forced to perform oral sex on her grandmother, after she'd just come out of a tub contaminated with her own urine. In fact, I hated it and often tweeted about my disgust to my fans during the process. Yet, I was determined not to make the same mistake I made with *Rainbow Heart*. I was not going to tailor Harmony's life experience to make my readers or me comfortable. Because quite honestly, readers don't want to be comfortable, they want their worlds rocked, and it's your job to rock them.

I must say this before we continue, being honest and explicit are not necessarily the same things. If you write a graphic book without writing the human side, it can come across as sadistic and vile. Honesty means staying true to the characters, whether good or bad.

Look, you are in the entertainment industry, _____. You are going to receive flack when your book is published, just like you receive flack in your everyday life. Please remember what your purpose is

THE END. PART 1

while penning your story. You want to whisk your readers away from their mundane lives, and into a world not of their own. Throw your readers into a wrecked storyline filled with emotion, and when you're ready, and only when you're ready, set them free.

Creative Exercise For The Day

What is the most heartbreaking moment of your novel so far? And how did you feel about writing it?

_____
_____
_____
_____
_____
_____

Notes:

_____
_____
_____
_____
_____
_____
_____
_____
_____
_____
_____
_____

DAY 6

"A writer who waits for ideal conditions under which to work will die without putting a word on paper."
-E B White

At this point you may find you're dealing with outside conditions and inside people. Your boyfriend wonders how much longer you'll be on your book, and if you want to go to the movies to see that film you were raving about. Your girlfriend calls you nonstop, and she's afraid you don't love her anymore; despite you making it clear that you'll be unavailable for 30 days early on. Your kids want you to play Michael Jackson *"The Experience"* on Wii, and you can't because you've set a goal that you really want to see through.

Suddenly, for a moment, when you hear the despair in your loved one's voices, you feel guilty about taking the time to do what you always wanted, and you wonder if now is the best time after all. Let me assure you, _____, that it is.

At the time this book was written, I have been successfully taking care of my family and myself for five years on writing. Meaning, there is no one in my home who is employed for any other organization but our own. I get up when I want. I sleep when I want and even hang out when I want.

I shamelessly shop for the labels I love like Gucci and Louis V. And push a Mercedes Benz just my size. I have a few stocks and bonds and I'm comfortable. Do you get the picture? I want you to think for a minute, how much time you will have for your family, if you took the time TODAY, to fulfill your dreams.

You don't have to be as shallow as me with what you spend your money on. In fact I don't even want you too. I'm still kind of young so I'm having lots of fun right now. However, I implore you to hold fast on giving up on writing your book this time. Whether you can see it or not, there is money in this business if you can consistently produce a quality product. *Quality* is the key! Anybody can write a book of trash. I certainly don't want you to become a writer *only* for the sake of money either. But, if you're doing something you love, shouldn't you get paid for it?

I notice a lot of books about publishing are afraid to tell you that money can be made in this business. Perhaps they don't want to make any promises that you can't achieve. I believe in the opposite. If a girl like me dropped out of high school in the ninth grade, and eventually received a GED, who also came from a violent background, tells you that money is in the business, you better damn sure believe that it is. Yes you will have to work up to that point, but that's what this book is trying to convey. I want you to push now and get into an empire state of mind. Work hard *now*, play harder *later*, is the motto I live by.

If you write a hot book, and you self-publish, you can earn money via the e-book market without having to go through a traditional publisher. (*Will discuss more in my upcoming novel, The End. Let That Be The Reason You Self-Publish*). What do you think will happen when you write more than one hot book? After awhile, you may even be able to replace your fulltime job!

So whether you are in it for the money or the glory, there will never be a better time to live out your dreams. The time is truly now. You've waited long enough. Cease the moment!

Creative Exercise For The Day

Sometimes your family and friends' reaction toward your work can also spark creativity. Think of the most recent time a loved one wanted to spend time with you, while you were busy writing your book. What kinds of things did they do to get your attention?

_____

_____

_____

_____

Now on the flip side, how did they make you feel?

_____

_____

_____

_____

Notes:

_____

_____

_____

_____

_____

_____

_____

_____

_____

_____

_____

DAY 7

"One of the great rules of art: Do not linger."
- Andre Gide

You're seven days in! I'm so proud of you. I bet you didn't think you could do it for so long did you? You are destined for greatness, _____. Welcome to the party!

At this point, you may also have the urge to rewrite your book. It's probably as irritating as a mosquito bump freshly made. I'm going to have to insist that you push forward. I'm also going to reiterate something I've been saying since the beginning. You cannot move forward, by walking backwards. Do not cheat yourself or this project. One of the main reasons people can't finish a book, is because they don't understand the importance of having a canvas first. The 30-day process is giving you your canvas.

Pushing forward and avoiding rewrites isn't just about working hard to get a complete book. It's also about jogging your creative energy. You will find over the next 23 days, maybe even now, that you are going to be flooded with so many ideas; you won't know what to do with yourself. If you've been listening to anything I say you should be writing them down on your note-taking device. However, moving forward and avoiding rewrites is the reason your creative muscles are flexing. You are on your way to becoming a published writer.

You may say, but Toy, I really do want to change one thing in my novel. Okay, let's take what you're saying into consideration. Let's also say you're writing, and you come to a part in your book in which you'd like to change something that you've already written. During the first 30, you are to write it on the *Note Sheet* section that we mentioned in Chapter Three and come back to it later. For example:

Make Shelly angry when her uncle talks about how weak her father was in chapter one.

When you are finished your 30-day challenge, you are to come back to the note, add it into your story, and place a check mark next to it when you're done on your sheet. This is the only way you can meet your deadlines and achieve your goals. Every single book I've written after *Rainbow Heart*, was written after I wrote my canvas.

Creative Exercise For The Day

Think of a time where you started something and didn't finish it. It could be a home improvement, going back to college or even sitting down and planning the vacation you always dreamed of. Describe how it made you feel to not follow through on that goal.

_____
_____
_____
_____

Now think about a time you started something and finished it. How did that make you feel?

_____
_____
_____
_____

THE END. PART 1

Notes:

_____
_____
_____
_____
_____
_____
_____
_____
_____
_____
_____
_____
_____
_____
_____
_____
_____
_____
_____
_____
_____
_____
_____
_____
_____

DAY 8

"The best rule for writing – as well as for speaking – is to use always the simplest words that will accurately convey your thoughts."
- David Lambuth

I need you for a moment to consider your favorite novel. If you have your GREAT book in front of you, thumb through it for a minute. Look at how the words flow on the page. Look at how the author creates his or her story. You'll find that some of the best writing utilizes the simplest words to make big statements. Let's look at the passage below.

Shelly's heart thwacked and oscillated because she envisaged the quandary frontward. Henceforth, the impression continued to occupy her mind.

Whatever you do, please don't pull out all of your million dollar words, and cram them into your book as if they would be unavailable at a later time. Readers aren't impressed with this move and it makes you look and sound pathetic. If you are writing a comedy, and you're looking for a laugh, then by all means do you, boo boo. In fact, feel free to record the foolish sentence I just quoted above also. You have my permission.

But if you truly care about your reader's experience, which you should be doing always, lighten up. I'm not asking you to dumb your readers down, _____, but I'm asking you to ease the load by making the message you are trying to convey clear. That same sentence could've been written as such:

THE END. PART 1

Shelly's heart thumped. She could clearly see danger coming her way. And later on, negative thoughts occupied her mind.

Creative Exercise For The Day

Sometimes using the same word can plague our work like polio can plague a child. Readers tire if you use the same words over and over. Think of a few words you run into the ground. There is no need to look over your work because you should know them by heart. What are they?

_____
_____
_____
_____
_____
_____
_____
_____

Using a Thesaurus, think of new words that can replace them.

_____
_____
_____
_____
_____
_____
_____
_____

Notes:

_____

_____

_____

_____

_____

_____

DAY 9

"I see the notion of talent as quite irrelevant. I see instead perseverance, application, industry, assiduity, will, will, will, desire, desire, desire."
- Gordon Lish

Am I more talented than a lot of writers? Yes. Can any writer with the will and desire reading this book surpass anything I've achieved so far? Of course! First of all I'm still working on my dreams, second of all people make writing harder than it has to be.

What separate's the greats from the flakes, in my opinion, is two different things. The greats have the dream and will to see things through. Will, in my opinion, is where many hopeful writers fall short. They'll come up with a great idea to write a book and the moment somebody says it's dumb, they'll scrap the entire project.

Too many people worry about what others think when planning and executing their life's dreams. I happen to be the cockiest person on the face of the earth. I refuse. No...let me run that back. I *wish a mothafucka would* get in the way of anything I plan to do in life.

Sorry to say, if you want to write this book, you have to be as arrogant as I am. By making your desires clear, and holding onto what you want by way of application, you will do this thing. If not, I feel sorry for you and your family. Why? Because you'll be bitter and angry at the world for the rest of your life.

At first you'll tell yourself the reason you didn't follow your dreams is because of your kids, work or your spouse. After time you may even start believing the madness. However, I am here to tell you, _____, that all of that will be a lie. In life, there is nothing worse than having a dream and not seeing it realized. You alone control what happens with your book and whether it will be completed or not. And its time you start to see this as truth.

Creative Exercise For The Day

Outside of writing this book, think of a future goal you're going to tackle. Write it down.

_____

_____

_____

_____

_____

_____

_____

Think of what you can do tomorrow, that doesn't interfere with the production of this book, to work on your goal.

_____

_____

_____

_____

_____

_____

Notes:

_____

_____

_____

DAY 10

"Don't be boring. Don't assume every thought you have is fascinating to others. Your job is to give people a reason to keep reading."
- Dave Barry

Authors do a great job of writing without considering the reader. And then they want somebody to buy their trash. In their minds, once the book is written, it should be worshipped and cherished. Some may go as far as to think that they could place their book next to the bible, and either or would be sufficient enough for prayer. "After all", they'll tell themselves, "I've achieved the impossible! I've written a book!"

When the book is published, and the responses are lack luster, they don't understand why. It's your job to make your characters shine, _____. This is why I didn't want you to use an outline. It's not that I don't believe that they will come in handy later in your journey. It's because using outlines often get you stuck on the plot and not the characters.

Remember, we aren't interested in just the speeding car chase. We are interested in who your characters are. And after some time, if you want to spend mental energy on the best chase scenes ever, you'll be well within your rights. If you do it correctly, your readers may hold their breaths praying that when the vehicle stops that their favorite characters will be alive and in tact.

How do you make characters pop? You paint their pictures! Lets look at the sentence below:

Shelly gripped the steering wheel.

The sentence isn't bad, but we don't care. You want your readers to fall in love with everything Shelly does. The simplest actions need to be an event. One of my favorite ways to do that is by using an analogy.

Shelly's hands gripped the steering wheel, as if it were the bar draping her legs, on a roller coaster ride.

People have seen the bar on rollercoasters and they can picture it in the example. So in their minds, they imagine how tightly she's holding on to the wheel, as if her life depended upon it. Always be in a visual state of mind. Its not your job to assume the readers will get the picture, you have to make them get it!

Creative Exercise For The Day

Think of two analogies and write them here.

_____

_____

_____

_____

_____

_____

_____

_____

DAY 11

"The character's attitude is more important than the plot."
- Stephen Cannell

Since we've started, I've been stressing the importance of building strong characters, in an effort to make a bestseller. Now on your 11th day, I want to go into a little more detail. As always, don't be concerned with going back and reading what you've already done. The object of this book is to practice restraint and learn new things as you go along, _____. Focus on building your knowledge about what it takes to write a book, before you rewrite. In order to explain characterization more clearly, lets talk about a few helpful hints.

You Build Strong Characters The Following Ways

- Dialogue
- Actions
- The clothing and the way it's worn
- The Character's physical attributes
- Through psychological attributes and their attitudes

Over the next few days, we will break down each point above. But today I want to discuss dialogue. For me, one of the easiest ways to make my characters unique is through dialogue. Let's take Shelly for instance in our story *Bad Pop Bad Cop*. Shelly is a kid who was thrust into the world and now she's in charge of convincing society that her father is innocent. If she were to be in conversation with Mark, her uncle and trusted police officer, the voices would be distinct.

"Did you do it?" Shelly asked, as she held the phone against her ear so harshly, the back of her earring stabbed the side of her neck. "I gotta know. Please."

"I told you, honey. I didn't do it. Now I know you hate to believe it, but your father is capable of many things. And in this instance, he was capable of rape and murder."

"But daddy wouldn't. He would never hurt my sister. He loved her too much."

"Honey, he did do it." He sighed. "Now why don't you come down to the precinct, and talk to me a little more. There are things you don't know about your father that I'd love to discuss with you in private. However, I'm gonna need to see that pretty face first. Besides, I miss my niece."

"My friend...she...she has the tape. She seen you leaving, uncle Mark. She seen your car."

If you notice in the dialogue above, Shelly sentences aren't as long as Mark's. In fact, she seems hesitant and nervous. It is clear that Shelly is not confident while Mark on the other hand is very aggressive.

When writing your dialogue ask yourself, will this character say this? At this point you should know more about your characters although there's still more to discover.

The key to characterization using dialogue is to remember who they are before writing down what they would say. Think about how you would feel if someone put words in your mouth that were not authentic. You would feel fake. This is exactly how your characters come across when you don't keep their uniqueness in mind.

THE END. PART 1

Creative Exercise For The Day

Think of two main characters in your book. Think about how different they are. Write a brief dialogue scene with them here.

_____

_____

_____

_____

_____

_____

_____

_____

_____

_____

_____

_____

Notes:

_____

_____

_____

_____

_____

_____

DAY 12

"Don't say the old lady screamed. Bring her on and let her scream."
- Mark Twain

It's easy to get stuck in a rut, _____.
But you are reading this book and using it as a companion along your journey to prevent this fatal state amongst writers. You particularly want to pay attention to this feeling when you're writing actions. For instance, to say a character walked, over and over in your book, can make it seem like your vocabulary is limited and that you are bored with your own work. If you are, how do you think your readers will feel? Having a thesaurus by your side can help with words you use often. I prefer the *Oxford American Writer's Thesaurus* although an online Thesaurus' will work just fine.

Instead of saying walk, challenge yourself to use a different word and sequence. Try to paint a picture that is extraordinary and stands out.

*Shelly **dawdled** toward her house. (To move slowly and idly)*
*Shelly **sauntered** toward Chance. (To move in a relaxed manner)*
Or even better:
*Shelly **plodded** toward Mark, as if she were carrying a sack of bricks on her back. (To walk doggedly and slowly)*

The idea is to come out of your usual way of doing things, to add spice to the ordinary.

Creative Exercise For The Day

THE END. PART 1

Think of five different ways to say your main character walked. Write them down.

_____
_____
_____
_____
_____
_____
_____
_____

Notes:

_____
_____
_____
_____
_____
_____
_____
_____
_____
_____
_____
_____
_____
_____
_____
_____
_____
_____

DAY 13

"And by the way, everything in life is writable about if you have the outgoing guts to do it, and the imagination to improvise."
- Sylvia Plath

The next way to make characters shine is through clothing. But if you fail, you'll not only irritate the hell out of the reader, you'll run the risk of a bad review (which you may get no matter how great your book is). For a long time I was guilty of this. And even to this day, I find myself falling back although I check myself quickly now. Do what I say, not as I do. You'll stay out of trouble that way.

When you describe clothing, _____, there are many things you must know. First, it is unnecessary to describe every piece of clothing a character is wearing unless it is crucial to your story.

Shelly wore blue jeans, a white shirt, black boots, her red leather jacket and her white hat.

The above sentence is a hot ass mess. But, by using a few pieces of clothing that you believe will give the reader an understanding of your character, and by working them into the storyline, readers will see them better.

The holes in Shelly's blue jeans seemed inappropriate for the winter storm brewing outside. So she took off her red leather jacket, and threw it over her knees for warmth.

By using the character's clothing, you can see how a picture is drawn which will keep your readers' attention longer.

THE END. PART 1

Creative Exercise For The Day

Using the following clothing pieces, write a description as if it were included in your storyline. Yellow pants, white t-shirt and red raincoat.

_____

_____

_____

_____

_____

_____

_____

_____

_____

_____

Notes:

_____

_____

_____

_____

_____

_____

_____

_____

_____

_____

_____

_____

_____

_____

DAY 14

"What I like in a good writer is not what he says, but what he whispers.
– Logan Pearsall Smith

It is no longer good just to say a man was black or white. In order for physical attributes to glow, one must hone in on other attributes as well. For instance, are there scars on their bodies? Does your character suffer from a debilitating disease, which leaves he or she with a limp?

In my novel *Redbone*, the main character suffered from an illness which had physical affects on her skin. The fear of this disease, and doing whatever she could to prevent the outward scars from appearing, caused her to act selfishly throughout the book.

I enjoy researching rare ailments and diseases. There are millions yet most of us will stick to things like Chicken Pox, Cancer and the like. Broaden your horizons, _____, and educate your readers about ailments they don't even know exist. They'll thank you with their loyalty.

Creative Exercise For The Day

Research bazaar diseases and think of ways to apply them in your story.

_____

_____

_____

_____

_____

_____

DAY 15

"To tell the story of the kid with the gun without telling the story of why he has it is to tell a kind of lie."
- Jay Z

There's nothing worse in my opinion, than to tell a story about death, violence and despair, without telling the readers how any of it occurred. In all of my books, I try my best to be sure to bring the reader up on the mentality of my characters. I don't want to forge an opinion; I just want to enlighten readers on who my villains are.

One of my most memorable characters is Madjesty Phillips. She is the daughter to a drunken whore, and also thanks to her abusive mother, spent her adolescent years believing she was a boy. As a young adult, she went about her life in a desperate attempt to find love. She would meet someone, lie about her sex, and fall in love at first sight. When the girls she dated discovered she was female, she'd beg and plead for them not to leave her.

Raunchy 2, in which this character is highlighted, goes into detail about her life in a way so graphic, even those who never heard about sexual identity disorder, can clearly understand how she came to be so desperate for love and acceptance. And why often times, she acted violent.

It is your duty as a writer, _____, to give your readers the proper background on your characters, without necessarily guiding their opinion. The worst thing you can do is have a character do something totally out of character, without an explanation or background. Your readers don't need to know everything you have planned for them, but if the character makes a move out of the ordinary, it must be justified.

Creative Exercise For The Day

Think about your main characters. What kind of parents
did they have? How did their parents treat them? Were they
abused? Think clearly and write your responses below.

_____
_____
_____
_____
_____
_____
_____
_____

Notes:

_____
_____
_____
_____
_____
_____
_____
_____
_____
_____
_____
_____
_____

DAY 16

"Fill your paper with the breathings of your heart."
- William Wordsmith

Let's talk about villains for a moment. I happen to love a good villain. Why? Because I believe when a writer creates the perfect villain, we discover that we have more in common than we thought otherwise. It doesn't mean we should justify crime or acts of violence. However, if we learn something from books, which we all should, perhaps we will move about life not being so judgmental.

In the past, villains were often thought of as monsters. You imagined their faces distorted or them being social outcasts. Although this is often true, the best villains look and act just like you and me. That's why when the world first saw Ted Bundy, an attractive and charismatic serial killer, they were confused. Their minds formed a picture of what a man responsible for killing over 35 victims would look like and they were definitely wrong.

It is important to understand, _____, that to create a good villain, you must give him two sides. In the early nineteenth century, it was okay to have a villain roaming about the earth, killing and maiming for no apparent reason. Remember, movies and TV shows were not as prevalent back then as they are now, and it was easy to horrify a person. Now the best villains must have many dimensions.

If your villain is a serial killer who murders elderly people for sport, perhaps you can make him a dog rescuer in his spare time. Or if your villain kidnaps children for profit, maybe she can be an advocate for change in Darfur. The point is to always make your villains both good and bad if you want to wow your audience. It'll pay off in the long run.

Creative Exercise For The Day

Think of the villain in your story. Give him both good and bad traits.

_____
_____
_____
_____
_____
_____
_____

Notes:

_____
_____
_____
_____
_____
_____
_____
_____
_____
_____
_____
_____

DAY 17

"If I don't write to empty my mind, I go mad."
-Lord Byron

Imagine what would happen if we took two opposing characters in your book and stuffed them in an elevator alone. What do you think would happen? Chances are, depending on the characters...someone might not come out alive.

One of the best techniques known to writers is the crucible. The crucible is *that thing* which holds your characters together. *That thing*, where no matter how hard they try, they can't walk away from. It is the desire for the characters to continue to fight although someone should call it quits. The crucible can be emotional or physical, as long as it is binding.

In our book *Bad Pop Bad Cop*, Shelly and Mark are involved in a crucible. Mark doesn't want to get in trouble with the law, and lose his career, and Shelly wants her father to be released from prison. So, the law is the crucible.

Also in our story, before Shelly's sister was murdered, the family was under tyranny by Shelly's father. No one could leave him or the house because they couldn't afford to take care of themselves. The need to be cared for and have security is the crucible.

By creating strong crucibles, you are likely to cause even more conflict and that's where the big bucks start rolling in!

Creative Exercise For The Day

Think about your characters. What crucible binds them together?

Notes:

DAY 18

"A writer's job is to tell the truth."
- Andy Rooney

This is a jewel so hear me closely, _____. I've mentioned before in this book to be sure to leave your readers hanging at the end of each chapter. Why? So that readers will continue to turn the pages. What I want to talk about now, is going to an entirely different location, after each cliffhanging chapter ends and the new one begins.

Using our story, consider the example below:

Chapter One – Chapter ends when Shelly learns that Mark may be involved in the murder of her sister. If I were to write a story, I would have Shelly sit in her uncle's car at the funeral. I would have her hug him and cry in his arms. When they separate, I would have her notice a necklace that belonged to Tiffany on the floor of his vehicle. The necklace would be significant because her sister would've received the necklace the night of the crime. Even though you want to know Shelly's reaction, I would close the chapter right there.

Chapter Two – Instead of going back to the funeral scene, I would open up the following chapter with Todd in prison. When the scene starts, he's having a conversation with an inmate name James, which is already tense because James is sizing Todd up. When another inmate whispers in James ear, he looks at Todd and asks is it true you raped your own daughter? The scene closes with no resolution.

Chapter Three – This chapter picks back up where Chapter one leaves off, as we find out how Shelly deals with discovering her sister's necklace. This chapter will also be left with a cliffhanger, and the cycle will continue until the book is complete.

It will take work and finesse, but once you have this technique down to a science, your readers won't have any choice but to finish everything you write.

Creative Exercise For The Day

Think about how you plan to start your story for the day. Think of ways to leave the reader hanging and where you'll end up in the chapter proceeding.

_____

_____

_____

_____

_____

_____

_____

_____

_____

_____

_____

DAY 19

"Writing is a socially acceptable form of schizophrenia."
- E. L. Doctrow

One quick way to have a reader toss your book, is by creating long drawn out chapters. The brain needs time to process what it's reading. If you write an entire page and it is not broken into paragraphs, you will irritate the hell out of your reader. And you'll get on my nerves too!

It is always best to write short chapters, _____. It gives the elusion that the story is moving along. This is one of the reasons people enjoy dialogue. Not only is dialogue interesting because it gives you insight on the characters, but also pages of dialogue push your story forward. Always remember that less is more and to break up your thoughts.

Paragraphs deal with specific themes and are indented. By learning to write good paragraphs, which organize your thoughts, your novel will be lucent. Using our story *Bad Pop Bad Cop*, let's say the main idea of our paragraph is to talk to Todd about his guilt or innocence. Let's look at our example below:

> *Shelly slogged toward the phone to speak to her father in prison. She needed to know if he was innocent or guilty before she put her life on the line, and defended his name. Although she planned to ask him directly, and await his answer, she would pay little attention to his response. She knew first hand that his mouth could lie but his eyes couldn't.*

The entire paragraph above is addressing Todd's innocence or guilt. If we were to also add in that paragraph, a few sentences about Shelly's day, it would not be an effective paragraph.

Creative Exercise For The Day

Think of the first paragraph you are going to write today. What is the main idea?

_____
_____
_____
_____
_____
_____
_____

Notes:

_____
_____
_____
_____
_____
_____
_____
_____
_____
_____
_____
_____
_____

DAY 20

"Show up. Get to work even when you don't feel like writing – especially when you don't feel like writing."
- Daniel H Pink

How are you, _____? Hopefully by now you have over one hundred or so pages. Please don't give up now because you're almost there. Do not underestimate the power of the first draft. There are many, *many* writers who have not come as far as you have today. I've seen them. *Many* of them. You will not be that kind of person. You can't. It's time to start building your financial security and you can do that by writing bestselling novels to build a solid bibliography.

If you keep a journal, go back to the day you started writing your book. Think about how excited you felt. Try to bring that energy over today. It is okay to feel sad, mad and happy at various stages during this project. What it is not okay to do is quit.

Creative Exercise For The Day

Think about how far you've come. Think about where you started. Do you feel more confident with your story?

_____
_____
_____
_____
_____
_____
_____
_____

What changed since you first started writing to make your storyline stronger?

_____

_____

_____

_____

_____

_____

_____

_____

What can you do to make your story better from this point on?

_____

_____

_____

_____

_____

_____

Notes:

_____

_____

_____

_____

_____

_____

_____

_____

DAY 21

"In good writing, words become one with things."
-Ralph Waldo Emerson

We covered a lot over the past twenty something days, _____. And yet I have another jewel I'd like to drop on you. There is another thing you should look for when writing your books, and that's avoiding placing the same word in the same paragraph repeatedly. In the past we talked about eliminating use of one particular word. What I'm speaking of now is slightly different. If you use the word walk in one paragraph, I want you to try your hardest not to use walk again in that paragraph. This won't always be possible but you should always try.

It gives the elusion that your vocabulary is weak and may bore your readers. Most readers won't know what bugs them about your work; they'll just give it a bad review. Its similar to tasting your favorite chocolate ice cream, and someone changing the brand to one you dislike. You don't understand what it is about the new ice cream that displeases you, because they're both chocolate. You just know you'll never order it again.

Let's consider the following paragraph:

*Shelly **walked** to the police precinct to file a report. She didn't want to, so she **walked** slowly. She felt like she was betraying her uncle, even though she was sure he was responsible for her sister's murder. When her stomach turned sour, she ran into the bathroom to regurgitate. When she got up the nerve to do what needed to be done, she **walked** back out.*

What about the above paragraph is redundant? If you guessed **walk** you are correct, even though I bolded the words to give you a hint. By deleting redundant words in the same paragraph, you perfect your craft and you ensure that your readers will receive a pleasant experience.

Creative Exercise For The Day

Look at a paragraph you wrote yesterday. Remember I said look *not* edit! Are there any words used more than twice in a paragraph? If so what are the words?

_____
_____
_____
_____
_____
_____
_____

Notes:

_____
_____
_____
_____
_____
_____
_____

DAY 22

"Budding authors, be self disciplined. It's a lonely job.
And listen to experts."
-Rosamunde Pilcher

If you've reached this far, _____,
you're disciplined and serious about your craft. We only
have a little further to go and the start of your journey will
be complete.

What I want to talk to you about today is a tool I
use that is to die for, in terms of efficiency and writing your
best book. I didn't mention it before now because I didn't
want you to use it. And even now as I tell you, I don't expect you to utilize this tool now. Instead, when you
FINISH your rewrites, I want you to consider this device.

The tool I'm speaking of is the text-to-speech tool. I
must tell you, that if ever there was a best-kept secret for a
writer, this is it. The reason being is because it's so easy to
miss key errors because you know what your story is supposed to say. Many times you ride past key inconsistencies
when editing whereas if you listened to it via a text-to-
speech application, you can hear your story and catch
flaws.

Most computers have this feature however; I also
use the one on my iPad and iPhone. It's called *SPEAK IT*. I
simply copy my work and paste it into the application, and
then I listen to what I've written. Hopefully by the time this
book is available, the *SPEAK IT* app is still on the market.
If it is not available for your phone, search for apps with
the same feature.

Another app I love is Dictionary.com. I set up noti-
fications so that I receive the word of the day. When the
notification pops on my phone, I try to incorporate it into

my daily page/word goal. This one tip helps increase my vocabulary and spices up my work.

Finally, because you are officially a writer, it is important that you think like one. The first thing you want to do is reserve your name at Godaddy.com. So if your name is James Brett you want to reserve www.jamesbrett.com. Even if you don't intend on using James Brett.com reserve it anyway, and also reserve the name you plan on using.

When you strike it big, the last thing you want is some domain stalker buying your name and holding it hostage until you give them an absorbent amount of money. Do yourself a favor. Reserve your name now!

Creative Thought For The Day

Research apps on your smart phone. What tools did you discover that could assist you on your journey?

_____

_____

_____

_____

_____

_____

_____

Notes:

_____

_____

_____

_____

_____

_____

DAY 23

Be a great troublemaker. It is your God given <u>write</u> as an author!
- T. Styles

Hopefully you avoid conflict in your personal life, _____. With you being an author, it is imperative that you have a sound mind and a peaceful lifestyle. I tell people quick, I cause trouble in my books but don't play it when it comes to my personal life. You must be diligent in that regard, which is why I suggested that you read both an interesting book in your genre and a positive non-fiction book to give yourself a peaceful state of mind when you're in the lab.

However, just because we are undisturbed creatures in the world, does not mean we should carry on in this way as writers. The best books will stress the hell out of your readers. Not because it's written poorly or carelessly, but because you are doing everything you can to build suspense and momentum. Only when you've made them pay dearly, do you let them off the hook and give them a brief break.

For instance, in our book *Bad Pop Bad Cop*, lets say Mark has located Shelly's whereabouts. And lets say she is trying to get away from him. The writer in us may write something like this:

Shelly ambled down the street until she spotted her uncle's unmarked car across the way. She remembered the vehicle from when he was over her house for a family function last year. So she slowly backs up, and runs away. However, Mark spots her anyway and rushes in her direction. Shelly jumps in her own car, and drives off with her life in tow.

As you can see we built up suspense and gave the reader a break immediately. What we should have written was this:

Shelly ambled down the street until she spotted her uncle's unmarked car across the way. She remembered it when he was over the house for a family function last year. So she backed up, in an effort to escape. However Mark saw her hesitancy, and got out of his vehicle to rush in her direction.

Shelly looks desperately for her car but she can't remember where she's parked. She can hear the sounds of his tennis shoes scratching the pavement clearer, which indicated he was close. She dipped behind a restaurant and pulls at the first door she finds. She nervously looks behind her to be sure he isn't near. Lucky enough to have a few more moments, she tugged at the door again but it is locked.

"Shelly! I'm gonna kill you!" Mark screamed, his voice assured her that he was dangerously close.

Shelly's heart rate increased until she noticed a wired fence ten feet ahead. She decided to take a chance and crawl up it. She was almost at the top until Mark grabbed her ankle ...

You get the picture? It is your job to avoid letting the reader off easily. Anything else is uncivilized.

Creative Exercise Of The Day

As you approach the ending of your 30 days, think about an action scene you have coming up. What can you do to drag the moment out to build suspense?

THE END. PART 1

_____
_____
_____
_____
_____
_____
_____
_____
_____

Notes:
_____
_____
_____
_____
_____
_____
_____
_____
_____
_____
_____
_____
_____
_____
_____
_____
_____
_____
_____
_____
_____
_____
_____
_____
_____
_____
_____
_____

DAY 24

"Great dialogue does not come from having a good ear for dialogue. It does not come from having some innate gift or talent for writing dialogue. It comes from this: knowing your characters so well that you know what they will say and how they will say it when faced with specific people, situations and events."
- Rob Tobin

Lets say I invited you out to eat. And let's say I wanted to talk to you about something. Let's also say the conversation went like this:

> *"Hello, _____."*
> *"Hello, Toy."*
> *"The sky is blue," I say.*
> *"I know. It is."*
> *"The moon comes out later tonight."*
> *"Why yes, Toy. It probably will."*
> *"I'm pretty sure if the cycle continues, the sun will be back out tomorrow too."*
> *"I believe you."*
> *"Hey...did I say the sky is blue?"*

I assure you that after awhile you would either say, I'm the most boring person you've met in your life, or that I have zero personality. Based on the dialogue above you'd be right.

If I haven't said it before let me say it here. Every sentence, every paragraph, every chapter must relate to the plot in one-way or another. It must. In the beginning, you don't need to worry too much. What I'm preparing you for now are the rewrites. Every sentence must enhance in some way, and that includes your dialogue.

THE END. PART 1

By the time you begin your rewrites, you will have a greater understanding of who your characters are. So if you happen upon a character who does not relate to the story, get rid of him. Don't let him impact your story negatively. You want to always be thinking, how does this apply to my story, when you begin rewrites. And although I want you to freestyle it now, thinking about the purpose of your chapters must be something you consider when your 30 days are up.

Dialogue should do the following for your novel:

Move the story forward
Give information
Contribute to characterization

If your dialogue is not contributing in any of the three ways during the rewrite process, scrap it and start all over again.

Creative Exercise For The Day

Think about the dialogue you are going to write today. Does it contribute to your overall storyline? If so how?

_____

_____

_____

_____

_____

_____

_____

_____

_____

Notes:

_____
_____
_____
_____
_____
_____
_____
_____
_____
_____
_____
_____
_____
_____
_____
_____
_____
_____
_____
_____
_____
_____
_____
_____
_____
_____
_____
_____
_____
_____

DAY 25

"A good novel tells us the truth about its hero; but a bad novel tells us the truth about its author."
– G. K. Chesterton

Before long you will learn to be smooth with your writing, _____. I like to say that you will develop a sort of swag, and your fans will be able to spot your work from miles away. One of the easiest ways to become stronger is by reading books on perfecting their craft.

I'm always amazed by authors who say they are the best in their field, when they never read other works or books on writing. A novelist should clearly be able to tell the difference between their first book and their second. They should also be able to tell the difference between their third and fourth. The only way to make this leap is by practicing and learning all you can in this field. Don't worry; I've included some of my favorite books in the resource section in the back but there are thousands out there.

Another way you can make your writing smooth is by getting rid of words that don't add to your storyline. I'm not going to lie, I often make this mistake myself. I must say, I'm way better than I was before. I definitely need work but don't we all.? I recorded a list of words below that unless they're used in dialogue to show characterization, you may need to avoid.

Just
I just thought you wanted to go to dinner with me.
Instead: I thought you wanted to go to dinner with me.

Really
You can really do a nice job by coming to work early.
Instead: You can do a nice job by coming to work early.

Quite
I'm quite irritated with you because of how you treated me yesterday.
Instead: I'm irritated with you because of how you treated me yesterday.

Perhaps
Perhaps if I take you to work, we'll have a few more moments to talk.
Instead: If I take you to work, we'll have a few more moments to talk.

That
I like the shirt that you wore yesterday.
Instead: I like the shirt you wore yesterday.

Had
I had thought about you before I got something to eat. That's why I called to see if you were hungry.
Instead: I thought about you before I got something to eat. That's why I called to see if you were hungry.

The dreaded 'Had Had'
He had had a bad day but to my knowledge, it got better.
Instead: He had a bad day but to my knowledge, it got better.

Creative Exercise Of The Day

Using the above list, think of ways you may incorrectly use the words, and then write a sentence without the word.

_____

_____

THE END. PART 1

_____
_____
_____
_____
_____
_____
_____
_____
_____
_____
_____
_____

Notes:

_____
_____
_____
_____
_____
_____
_____
_____

DAY 26

"The most important thing to remember is to choose a title that depicts what your book is about. Not the title you thought of driving on the way to work."
- T. Styles

Let's talk about titles for a moment, _____.
If you do nothing else, you must do this, choose a title that gives the reader an idea of what your book is about. In my opinion, and since you're reading this book you must want it, titles are as important to a book as the storyline. You need three things above all, a hot book cover, title and novel. Let's look at a few of my titles.

Raunchy – *about a mother who is an alcoholic and sex addict.*

Shyt List – *about a woman who believes she was wronged by the people she loved so she created a list of names to seek revenge.*

Black & Ugly – *about a young girl who was called black and ugly all her life because of her dark skin.*

The Face That Launched A Thousand Bullets – *about a girl whose beauty is so intoxicating, she causes a war between two friends.*

You need to consider names that give the reader a glimpse of what your book is about. You don't need a title when you start the book but it's a good idea to brainstorm each day and record a list of possibilities. Often the name will come to you in dialogue, or when you're out and about. Do this everyday, or as often as you can, and the right title will eventually call your name.

Creative Exercise Of The Day

Think of some titles that will effectively give the reader a glimpse of what your book is about. Record them here.

_____
_____
_____
_____
_____
_____
_____
_____
_____
_____

Notes:

_____
_____
_____
_____
_____
_____
_____
_____
_____
_____
_____
_____

DAY 27

"Action, reaction, motivation, emotion, all have to come from characters. Writing a love scene requires the same elements from the writer as any other."
-Nora Roberts

I hated writing love scenes.
Now I love writing love scenes.
But I hate writing sex scenes.
After all, they're unnecessary.
When I first started my career, I was the worst at writing sex scenes. Even to this day I shy away from them. In order for me to be able to effectively write sex scenes, I have to care about the characters in some way. This is probably why most of my stories are very passionate, to a point where it can be perceived as violent once the sexual encounter finally happens. The reason being, I take my characters through the ringer before I allow them to be intimate. It's a lot of fun, _____.

There are times my readers will believe two love interests are about to be passionate, only for me to make them fight, causing them to be pushed further apart. This is how you build strong love stories. Even if you're writing erotica, you should keep your characters from having sex as long as possible before their moment arrives.

A love scene embodies more than just sex between lovers. You must give the illusion that time is not on their side. If two people can get together and have sex anytime they want, where is the romance? Where is the passion?

Create the impression that the two shouldn't be together. Are they cheating? Is one of the lovers getting married the next morning? Is one of the lovers moving out of the country and will never see the other again? Is somebody being drafted to the army?

THE END. PART 1

Before the love scene takes place, did you build a strong enough desire for the character or characters to need love? Is there foreplay leading up to the love scene? For instance dancing at a dim nightclub, a soothing massage or maybe even a passionate kiss. These are just a few of the things you need to consider, before penning intimate moments.

Creative Exercise Of The Day

Think of ways you can enhance desire before the intimate moments in your book. Make sure these moments do not include intercourse.

_____
_____
_____
_____
_____
_____
_____

Notes:
_____
_____
_____
_____
_____
_____
_____

DAY 28

"Know how you're going to end your story before you start writing; without a sense of direction, you can get lost in the middle."
- Joan Nixon

Hopefully you've considered your ending up to this point, _____. Besides, in a few days your rough draft will be over. If you haven't thought of the ending to die for, don't kill yourself. Remember that you have a re-write coming and it will be a perfect time to consider it then.

Also before you start your rewrites, consider the four items below.

1. *The Resolution* – *THE ENDING*
2. *The Beginning* – *THE SETUP*
3. *Inciting Incident* – *THE CIRCUMSTANCE THAT CREATES MAIN TENSION*
4. *Lock In* – *PROTAGONIST MUST CARE FOR THE CIRCUMSTANCE*

The Resolution: How will your story end? Will there be a sequel? Will they live happily ever after? Knowing the ending will allow you to set up every chapter so that the moments can line up.

The Beginning: Did you grab your reader? Did you use an epigraph or create an air of illusion. Whatever you do, make sure it's interesting enough to hold your reader hostage.

THE END. PART 1

Inciting Incident: What issue causes the drama? In our story *Bad Pop Bad Cop*, the inciting incident is the murder of Shelly's sister. What is your inciting incident?

Lock In: Why must the protagonist be the one to seek resolution? In our story Shelly's sister was murdered and her father was convicted. Her mother is too weak to fight back and she has evidence that her uncle may be involved. So, Shelly is the only one who can seek justice.

This above process should take no more than an hour to come up with, as it may change slightly as you continue with your storyline. During the rewrite process, if you need an outline then, it is definitely acceptable.

Creative Exercise Of The Day

Reviewing the components above, which do you believe will be more difficult for you and why?

_____
_____
_____
_____
_____
_____
_____
_____
_____
_____

DAY 29

"I am neither a man nor a woman but an author."
- Charlotte Bronte

When you write, you must convince people that you are all things. If you are writing about a child, you must be child-like and innocent. If you are a man you must consider how you'd interact with other people, particularly women. What are your body mechanics like? Are you a follower or a leader? If you are a woman you must consider the things that embody femininity, assuming she is feminine. If she's aggressive you must do an accurate job depicting these traits too.

At the end of the day, it is your duty to be all things, _____. If you run into a topic that you are unsure about, do your research. Let's say for instance you are writing about a lesbian couple and the lovers are preparing to have sex. Let's also say that you are a straight man who is in a committed relationship with a woman. It may be difficult for you to write about this scene with honesty, *if* you are not open-minded. So do the research. Read blogs. If you have lesbian friends ask them if you can interview them.

When I was writing, *Miss Wayne & The Queens Of DC*, a novel about a flamboyant gay man, I was able to secure many interviews for my novel simply by joining gay forums and asking for them. I was overwhelmed with how welcoming the community was. It was important to them that I got the lifestyle down correctly and I felt a sense of duty after speaking to them to be honest. The last thing you want to do is create inaccurate depictions in your novel. You don't want to be insensitive. It is your duty to get it right and write it better!

THE END. PART 1

Creative Exercise For The Day

Think about a character in your novel that is unlike you. Are you creating fair depictions?

_____
_____
_____
_____
_____
_____

If not, what can you do to change it?

_____
_____
_____
_____
_____
_____

Notes:

_____
_____
_____
_____
_____
_____
_____
_____

DAY 30

"There is no greater agony than bearing an untold story inside of you."
- Maya Angelou

AMAZING!!!!
YOU DID IT!
CONGRATULATIONS, _____!
If you made it this far, after today, you'll have a complete first draft in your possession! Today you will officially become an author! I am truly proud of you because you set a goal and was determined to keep it. When you're done, take a look at your work. Pick it up and hold it closely to you. This may seem weird at first but to me it makes perfect sense. You have effectively put together a story that once complete will reach millions.

Getting into a gratitude state of mind is powerful. You want to always be sending out well wishes whenever you write to your readers. I don't care if you write Horror or Christian fiction. The purpose of your novel is to provide an escape so readers will feel your love. God is truly in the details.

So as you sit down to write for the day, take a second to imagine your reader. See her skimming through hundreds of books at a local bookstore, seeking the perfect pick. Imagine she picks up one book, reads the back, frowns and places it down. Then imagine she selects another, reads the binder and shakes her head before returning it to its place. Then imagine she happens upon your book, *Bad Pop Bad Cop.*

She reads the binder and is immediately taken by your title. When another reader ambles down the isle, your reader snatches the book because it's the only one left. She flips the book over and the synopsis has her immediately.

THE END. PART 1

She turns the cover around and even the image is appealing and interesting. She opens the book to the first page, and is almost knocked backwards upon reading your first sentence. She's a speedy reader, so she's able to finish the first page before she even makes it to the register.

She pays for her purchase and reads a few more paragraphs as she walks toward her car. She's so engrossed in your work of art that she accidently bumps into an elderly couple on their way into the store. She apologizes repeatedly before dodging to her car to prevent hurting anybody else.

Without putting her key into the ignition, she reads the first chapter, and then the second. She tells herself she'll only read one more, but before she knows it, she's on chapter five. She is fully prepared to read more, until her husband calls and asks if she's okay. It's only then that she realizes its nighttime. She hurries home so she can take a bath and pick up where she left off.

This is what you must be thinking about when you rewrite your book. The reader. Be considerate of the reader and be considerate of life and the circumstances going on around you. Remember to be an honest writer. The best writers are perceptive and aware of everything and everybody. If you are so self-absorbed that you can't consider anyone else, you will not be good in this game. I promise you. But if you're reading this book, I have no doubt that you care enough to do your very best!

Creative Exercise For The Day

Imagine a reader picking up your book in a library. Based on what you've written now, what do you think will shock them the most?

_____
_____
_____
_____
_____
_____
_____
_____
_____

Notes:
_____
_____
_____
_____
_____
_____
_____
_____
_____
_____
_____
_____
_____
_____
_____
_____

CHAPTER EIGHT

I wrote my book. Now what?

"Relax, darling! You've written a book!"
-T. Styles

You've finished your rough draft and now what? You walk away for a week and go back to your life! You hang out with your friends at your favorite bar. You go to the zoo with your children, or take them to the amusement park. You hang out with your spouse and catch a movie; afterwards you go to an upscale restaurant before returning home to make love. You call your parents and make sure they're okay and you catch up with old friends.

I must warn you. You will find that going on with your life will be easier said than done. While hanging out with friends, you'll be approached by a loser. His breath will stink so badly, it'll remind you of a dead animal on the side of the road. This time, you'll be intrigued and may even give him a few minutes of your time.

You look at his bad haircut. The wrinkles in his pants. The way he nervously rubs his chin in an attempt to be cool. You focus on his eyes, and how they seem to rest everywhere but on your face. Like your breasts and your lips. After he pimps away, you'll grab your phone. But instead of storing his number as you promised, you record his unique characteristics, maybe even his name in your book notes. This is the life of an author.

It takes thirty days to make and break a habit. Thirty days my friend. You have teased your creative muscles for a month and now they are working for you. You can't let an interesting moment go if you tried. You're like a reporter of life.

I can't remember the last time I've been able to sit down in a conversation without analyzing what's being said and what's not being said. I'm not judging...I'm analyzing. There's a difference. I'm an excellent listener and some people say I give superb advice. Whatever is said about me, I know that I am not normal. I am not an average person, nor do I want to be, and you aren't either.

Think about the people in and around your life. Think about the friends who will let you talk for an hour, without interrupting you once, because they really care about what you have to say. If you are like normal people, you probably don't have many associates like this in your life. Now think about yourself. What kind of friend are you? And what kind of friend can you be?

We have a responsibility to be present. We have a responsibility to care about others. We have a responsibility to care about life. Our reward? To some it may seem like nothing but to those who tell stories, it is everything. Our reward for being present, and having open hearts and ears, is that we will forever be connected to something greater than ourselves. People gravitate to us not because we're writers, but because we have the ability to make them feel alive. Because unlike some, when you operate as a present author, you become connected to Source or God. You become connected to humanity and as a result, you'll lead a fuller life.

So don't be alarmed if things are not the same when you return to your world after writing your novel. Because once you're an author you will never lead a normal life again.

Embrace the fact that your characters will talk to you while you're holding your baby. They'll whisper in

THE END. PART 1

your ear when you are intimate with your loved ones. And they'll groove with you while you're on the dance floor with your friends. Welcome, my sister and brother in pen! The world has been waiting on you, and I'm happy you gave me the honor of leading the way.

Notes:

_____
_____
_____
_____
_____
_____
_____
_____
_____
_____
_____
_____
_____
_____
_____
_____
_____
_____
_____
_____
_____

CHAPTER NINE
The First Draft

"The First Draft Of Anything Is Shit"
- Ernest Hemingway

Okay you've enjoyed your time with your family and friends. Like I promised new ideas and subplots infiltrated every waking moment. And since you're my student I know you've written them down. You may have more additions to contribute to your budding story. Great!

First things first, go to Chapter Five and reread the Hero's Journey. Understand it and think of ways to apply it to your story. Then pull out the charts you used in the beginning and scan over your information. This will allow you to remember who your characters are. What are their quirks? What things do they love and hate? Who are the people around them that impact their lives?

Once you've analyzed your charts, take your manuscript out and add it into your computer. You'll find that you'll be doing changes as you go along. Its okay. These are rewrites. Although you can mill over chapters you are not to spend more than a day on five pages. I want you to keep the pace you're accustomed to and stay within 30 days. Grant it, you won't have to spend as much time making things up because you already have your foundation. But keep the pace.

Let's go over a few tips and refreshers below:

THE END. PART 1

Tips & Refreshers

1. Reserve your name as a domain. When you make it famous, and you will, you don't want to be forced to pay someone an absorbent amount of money when you're ready to build your website. I use Godaddy.com for my domain name and Davida Baldwin at Odd Ball Designs for my book covers. She is amazing and can be reached at www.oddballdsgn.com.

2. Be cognizant of punctuation after your first draft. If used incorrectly it can change the entire meaning of a sentence. One of my favorite examples is the following:
   - *Woman without her man is nothing.*
   - **Now look:** *Woman; without her, man is nothing.*

3. Be a great listener. You'll make the best writer and you'll be an even better friend.

4. Remember that whether you write a great book or not, you won't be able to please everyone. Just write the best book possible and you'll please most.

5. When you complete all your rewrites, read your entire book aloud or use a text to speech device. You'll be able to pick up on errors you won't see with your eyes alone. After all, your mind knows what your book is supposed to say but your ears don't.

6. If you delete a scene, save it in a file called 'Deleted Scenes'. Although it might not work out for your current project, it may do wonders for your next book.

7. It is unnecessary to say *he said* or *she said* in every sentence. By using an action sentence after dialogue, the reader will understand immediately who is talking.
   - Ex. "I don't want to be bothered." Shelly walked away leaving him alone.

8. Join the, The End support group. Meet other writers in your journey. Site: http://groups.yahoo.com/group/theendnovelin30days/

9. Try, try, and try to find unique names. Readers love them!

10. If you are easily distracted by the Internet, like most people are, disconnect the Wi-Fi while working on your book.

   I've included some excellent books you may use to help you with this task in Resources. Use them because they'll help you greatly!
   Well get started! Time is of the essence! I'm so proud of you!

The End. How To Write A Bestseller In 30 Days **is the first in a series. Complete the series with the following editions.**

THE END. Making Your Rewrites Shine

THE END. Let That Be The Reason You Self Publish

THE END. Dangerous Publishing Contracts

(COMING SOON)

GREAT WEBSITES FOR WRITERS

Merriam Webster Online
www.merriam-webster.com
This site offers a dictionary, thesaurus, and encyclopedia.

Narrative Voice
en.wikipedia.org/wiki/Narrative_mode
Review this page to determine how to use narrative voices.

Bartleby
www.bartleby.com
This site is excellent for quotes.

Google Books
http://books.google.com/
An excellent resource to find phrases, free books, passages and other information for your novel.

Wikipedia
www.wikipedia.org
My all time favorite site. You can virtually find anything you're looking for here. A must have resource for writers.

Cha Ching
www.chacha.com
An excellent resource, which is powered by human beings. Ask these specialists anything you want!

Library of Congress
www.loc.gov/library/libarch-digital.html
Offers access to an online library. There are currently over 100,000 titles available

The Internet Public Library
www.ipl.org
A resource for newspapers, magazines, periodicals, etc. A must have to check your facts when writing your novel.

InfoPlease
www.infoplease.com
Another resource to get your most pressing questions answered.

Writers Digest
www.writersdigest.com
Arguably the most important site available for writers. It offers resources on becoming a great writer and getting published.

Writing.Com
www.writing.com
This site is free and offers a place for your portfolio, contests information, activities and other tools.

The OWL (Online Writing Lab)
owl.english.purdue.edu
Has over 200 high quality grammar and writing resources.

Publishing Law Center
www.publaw.com
Copyright, Trademark law.

About.com
fictionwriting.about.com
Publishes a guide to fiction writing with general information about fiction

NaNoWriMo
www.nanowrimo.org
National Novel Writing Month challenges writers to push out their books in 30 days. This is done every year in November. Excellent resource!

Book In A Week
www.book-in-a-week.com
If you really want to test the limits, Book In A Week gives you the resources to get your novel done in seven days.

Baby Names
www.babynames.com
Tired of James, Ann, Melissa and Tom? Expand your horizons by checking out some great names via this site.

Agent Query
agentquery.com
Not interested in self-publishing? Need an agent? Check out a few here!

Oddball Designs
www.oddballdsgn.com
Need a great book designer? Want to have your cover stand out from the rest? Seek the best.

ALL TIME FAVORITE BOOKS

Bird by Bird
Anne Lamott

Stein On Writing
Sol Stein

Stephen King On Writing
Stephen King

The Book Of Awakening
Mark Nepo

How To Grow A Novel
Sol Stein

THE CARTEL PUBLICATIONS TITLES
COMPLETE LIST
www.thecartelpublications.com

Shyt List
Shyt List 2
Shyt List 3
Shyt List 4
Shyt List 5
Pitbulls In A Skirt
Pitbulls In A Skirt 2
Pitbulls In A Skirt 3
Pitbulls In A Skirt 4
Pitbulls In A Skirt 5
A Hustler's Son
A Hustler's Son 2
Black & Ugly
Black & Ugly As Ever
Poison
Poison 2
Hell Razor Honeys
Hell Razor Honeys 2
Victoria's Secret
The Unusual Suspects
La Famila Divided
Year Of The Crackmom
Dead Heads
Reversed
Quita's Dayscare Center
Raunchy 1
Raunchy 2
Raunchy 3
The Face That Launched A Thousand Bullets
Lipstick Dom
Luxury Tax

CARTEL PUBLICATIONS
PRESENTS

The Cartel Collection
Established in January 2008
We're growing stronger by the month!!!
www.thecartelpublications.com

Cartel Publications Order Form
Inmates <u>ONLY</u> get novels for $10.00 per book!

Titles		*Fee*
Shyt List	_____	$15.00
Shyt List 2	_____	$15.00
Pitbulls In A Skirt	_____	$15.00
Pitbulls In A Skirt 2	_____	$15.00
Pitbulls In A Skirt 3	_____	$15.00
Victoria's Secret	_____	$15.00
Poison	_____	$15.00
Poison 2	_____	$15.00
Hell Razor Honeys	_____	$15.00
Hell Razor Honeys 2	_____	$15.00
A Hustler's Son 2	_____	$15.00
Black And Ugly As Ever	_____	$15.00
Year of The Crack Mom	_____	$15.00
The Face That Launched a Thousand Bullets		
	_____	$15.00
The Unusual Suspects	_____	$15.00
Miss Wayne & The Queens of DC		
	_____	$15.00
Year of The Crack Mom	_____	$15.00
Familia Divided	_____	$15.00
Shyt List III	_____	$15.00
Raunchy	_____	$15.00
Raunchy 2	_____	$15.00
Reversed	_____	$15.00
Quita's Dayscare Center	_____	$15.00

Please add $4.00 per book for shipping and handling.
The Cartel Publications * P.O. Box 486 * Owings Mills * MD * 21117

Name: _____

Address:_____

City/State:_____

Contact # & Email:_____

Please allow 5-7 business days for delivery. The Cartel is not
responsible for prison orders rejected.

CARTEL URBAN CINEMA

WWW.CARTELURBANCINEMA.COM